Coaching Swimming Effectively

The American Coaching Effectiveness Program
Level 1 Swimming Book

Jean G. Larrabee

Human Kinetics Publishers, Inc.
Champaign, Illinois

Library of Congress Cataloging-in-Publication Data

Larrabee, Jean G.
Coaching swimming effectively.

Bibliography: p.
1. Swimming—Coaching. I. Title
GV837.65.L37 1987 797.2'1 86-18594
ISBN 0-87322-080-3

Developmental Editor: Steve Houseworth
Copy Editor: Kevin Neeley
Production Director: Ernie Noa
Typesetter: Theresa Bear
Text Design: Julie Szamocki
Text Layout: Denise Mueller
Illustrator: David R. Bush
Cover Design: Jack Davis
Printed By: Versa Press

ISBN 0-87322-080-3

Printed in the United States of America

10 9 8 7 6 5 4 3 2 1

Human Kinetics Publishers, Inc.
Box 5076, Champaign, IL 61820

Series Preface

Coaching Swimming Effectively is part of the American Coaching Effectiveness Program (ACEP) Level 1 sport-specific series. The decision to produce this series evolved after the release of the ACEP Level 1 sport science course. In that course local youth sport administrators were encouraged to apply the information presented to the specific sports in their program. They were asked to identify the skills to be taught and the proper progression in teaching these skills. They were also asked to develop a seasonal plan and sample practice plans for their coaches.

The task seemed easy enough, but it was not. Considerable time is needed to carefully identify the skills to be taught and then to put them into a seasonal plan from which daily practice plans can be derived. As a result, the ACEP staff were encouraged to develop this information from various sports which we now have done.

The ACEP LEVEl 1 sport-specific series is unique in several ways.

1. The emphasis is on *teaching* skills to athletes, not on how to learn the skills yourself, as in most other books.
2. The emphasis also is on teaching basic skills to beginning athletes. Often, they will be very young children, but not always. Therefore, the books in this series are developed for coaches who teach the basics to children from 6 to 15 years of age.
3. Careful consideration is given to the proper *progression* for teaching these skills. Information from the field of motor development is combined with practical experience of veteran coaches to ensure that the progressions maximize learning and minimize the risk of injury.
4. *Seasonal* plans for the teaching of basic skills are presented along with *daily practice plans* for three age groups. Coaches will find these plans very helpful.
5. Drills or exercises appropriate for beginning athletes are also included.

Three other helpful features appear in each book in this series: A short history of the sport to help you appreciate the evolution of the game, a glossary of terms, and the rules of the sport are provided.

PRACTICAL, BASIC, and ACCURATE were the guiding principles in preparing this series. The content had to be practical for beginning coaches and yet equally useful for more experienced coaches. Coaches did not need another treatise on the sport; many of those are already available.

Keeping this series basic was perhaps the most difficult task. Including more information about the skills to impress coaches with all the knowledge available was constantly tempting. However, we resisted because this is not what coaches of beginning athletes need.

Finally, accuracy was essential; thus, many expert coaches and sport scientists reviewed the content of the book to confirm its accuracy.

To achieve maximum benefit, the books in this series cannot be read in an evening and then be put aside. They must be used like a reference book, a dictionary, or a working manual. Read the book thoroughly; then refer to it often during the season.

This book and ACEP are dedicated to the purpose of improving the quality of youth sports. We hope you will find the books in the series useful to you in achieving that goal. Enjoy your coaching, and thanks for helping young people learn to play sports better.

Rainer Martens, PhD
ACEP Founder

Contents

List of Drills and Exercises

Preface

This manual is designed for swimming coaches whose teams train during a season running from two to six months each year, engage primarily in dual meets, and swim an adjusted format of events stressing the shorter distances. Swimmers of teams that fit this description are commonly referred to as "recreational swimmers."

I have attempted to include only the basic materials relevant to coaching at the recreational level. To determine the topics that would be most helpful to coaches, I used a questionnaire to solicit the opinions of coaches who have worked with recreational swimmers at some time during their careers. Twenty of the coaches responding had worked with both recreational and year-round teams, and twenty had worked with only recreational teams. The experiences of both groups of coaches and what they had learned from their swimmers helped to establish the content of this manual.

I believe that a coach in a recreational situation has three major goals:

1. To create a healthy and enjoyable environment for the swimmers.
2. To teach the swimmers to swim strokes legally as specified by the National High School Federation with appropriate starts and turns.
3. To improve the swimmer's performance through better stroke techniques and developing enough endurance to maintain the use of the proper techniques.

This manual presents only the information vital to coaching at the recreational level in order to help the novice coach to achieve all three goals in one short season. Questions are interspersed throughout the manual to help you check your comprehension and to allow you to consider the application of important points to your particular teams. Typical answers are included at the end of the manual. A glossary of swimming terms is also provided at the end of the manual for your information.

Jean Larrabee

Acknowledgments

The author wishes to express appreciation to Dr. Kathryn Luttgens for her continued support, suggestions, and valued comments; to Janet Swanson for her technical expertise; and to John Larrabee for his patience and proofreading.

Swimming Coaching Guide

Welcome to swimming! You have joined the estimated 3 million other coaches who make youth sports possible in the United States. Whether you are a volunteer or a paid coach, you have the opportunity to make a tremendous contribution to the development of your young athletes. Furthermore almost half a million young people annually swim competitively.

People coach for many different reasons: Some coach because they love sports; some because they enjoy working with young people. Others coach because they have a son or daughter who will play on the team. These are all good reasons to coach. In fact, no matter why you choose to coach, taking the time to help young athletes learn to swim is an important contribution to their development and, consequently, to your community.

So now you are facing the upcoming swimming season. Have you coached swimming before? Have you thought about what you plan to do? Have you ever worked with beginning swimmers? Do you know how to teach specific strokes and techniques? If the answer to any of these questions is no, then you will want to read this book carefully. If you are determined to help your swimmers have a positive and successful experience, and if you take the time to study *Coaching Swimming Effectively*, then you will be on your way to a successful season.

It is important for every coach to establish a coaching philosophy, for this philosophy will help you determine (a) your goals, or what you want to accomplish, and (b) how you will accomplish these goals. You may want to consider one of two major coaching philosophies: You might choose to emphasize winning as the most important objective, or you might stress participation, fun, and skill development as the most important objective.

The philosophy advocated through the American Coaching Effectiveness Program is *Athletes First—Winning Second*. By this statement we mean that every decision you make as a coach should first be in the best interest of your athletes, and second in the desire to win. We hope that helping young people to develop physically, psychologically, and socially will always be more important to you as you coach than beating the other team.

Athletes First—Winning Second does not mean winning is unimportant, or said more accurately, that striving to win is unimportant. You should instill in your swimmers a desire to win, to strive to do their best, to pursue excellence. However, the outcome of the game—the winning or losing—is not the most important objective. The most important objective is that your swimmers try their best. If they do their best, they will have been successful—regardless of the outcome of the contest.

This philosophy also will be reflected in how you present yourself to the players on your team. As a coach, you are in an influential position, Thus, how you teach will be as important as what you teach. To implement the ACEP philosophy, consider the following points:

Be a good role model. Present a model for behavior you want your athletes to emulate. Set positive examples at practices and games.

Everyone is important. Treat each swimmer as an important human being. Each person will have a different personality and different needs. Be sensitive to these differences and show interest and concern for each team member.

Consider the age and skill levels of your swimmers. Your athletes will be full of energy and eager to try many skills. However, they may also be young and not yet capable of performing as adults. This means you must approach your athletes at their level. Do not expect them to come up to your level.

Consider individual differences. Teach swimming skills according to the ability of each swimmer. Some will be fast learners with whom you can progress rapidly. Others will not learn as quickly, so you will need to proceed more slowly with them.

Keep everyone active. Organize your practices and meets so that each swimmer is able to participate as much as possible. Young people want to swim for many reasons, one of the most important being to have fun participating. If they are not kept active in practices or allowed to compete in meets, they will quickly lose interest.

Include athletes in the decision-making process. As a coach you should help lead your athletes to an understanding of the skills, strategies, and tactics they need to develop. Listening to your athletes and suggesting several options to develop sport skills is a great way to do this. Naturally, young athletes should not control the entire practice, but do consider their interests and ideas when designing practices and planning meets.

Be patient. You will need to have patience with beginning swimmers who are learning strokes. Swimming skills require timing, coordination, and body control that can only be developed through repeated practice. Encourage your athletes to develop their skills, and positively reinforce them for their effort and skill development. When young swimmers learn new skills, both you and they should be proud.

Chapter 1: Evolution of the Racing Strokes

Competitive swimming was first developed in England during the late 1830s when contests were held in six pools located around London. The breaststroke was the preferred stroke as people attempted to imitate the motions that propel the frog with such speed. As man searched for a more efficient stroke, he turned onto his side and then lowered resistance by lifting one arm out of the water in the overarm sidestroke as shown in Figure 1-1.

Fig. 1-1

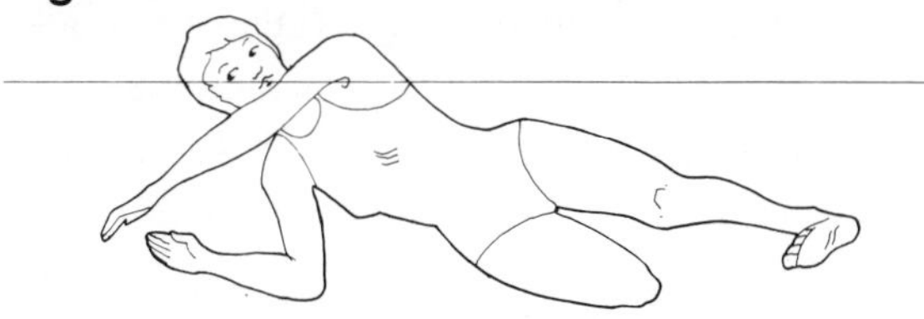

In 1873, John Trudgen introduced a double hand-over-hand stroke learned from South American Indians. This "trudgen crawl" stroke remained in vogue for 25 years until attention turned to the legs. The Australian Richard Cavill then won the International Championships using an up-and-down leg action combined with the hand-over-hand crawl stroke (see Figure 1-2).

American swimming coaches made further refinements in the breathing and kicking techniques of the crawl. In 1906 C.M. Daniels used these refinements to swim a world record time of 55.4 seconds in the 100-yard freestyle, and the American crawl stroke became the favored style.

Fig. 1-2

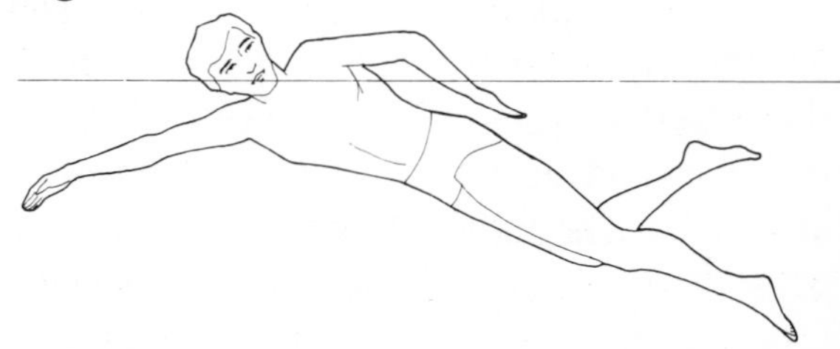

In the 1924 and 1928 Olympic Games, Johnny Weissmuller added breathing and body position innovations that allowed him to set a world record of 51.0 seconds. This record was to stand for 20 years.

Following its recognition as a competitive event by the International Swimming Federation (ISF) in 1912, the backstroke's development paralleled that of the crawl stroke. It was first swum as an inverted breaststroke and later with a double overarm recovery. Final modifications of an up-and-down kicking motion and alternating hand-over-hand arm action made the backstroke the second-fastest stroke.

The breaststroke, now the slowest stroke, remained a competitive event. It was the only stroke with a prescribed style similar to that required of breaststrokers today. A variation of this style was proposed by David Armbruster, coach at the University of Iowa, in 1934. He devised a double overarm, out-of-the-water recovery that was used by breaststrokers until the late 1950s. At that time, the dolphin or fishtail kick was legalized for competition, thus separating the butterfly and the breaststroke into two distinct strokes.

The research and literature influencing swimming in the United States between 1930 and 1950 stressed survival skills as well as stroke efficiency in the water. The American National Red Cross, YMCA, and Boy Scouts of America were the recognized swimming authorities of the time. College coaches served as consultants to these organizations, and they published swimming books emphasizing the racing strokes. However, all favored the methods originally intended for survival swimming.

One example of the swimming literature of the 1960s is the *Aquatics Handbook* by Gabrielson, Spears, and Gabrielson (1968), who recognized that different types of coaches need special information and included a chapter on competitive swimming. The authors, however, described the freestyle armstroke as the same alternating overarm pull that was employed in the Australian crawl at the turn of the century.

Concurrently, this idea was being questioned by Dr. James Counsilman of the University of Indiana. Counsilman spent years attempting to train his competitors to swim in the conventional manner, but he found that the most talented swimmers had trouble with the accepted approach. Through stop action photographs of successful swimmers, Counsilman attempted to determine the most efficient way to swim fast. He added to his knowledge by consulting Australian Olympic Coach Forbes Carlisle and coaches of other sports at the University of Indiana regarding the development of methods for training, tapering, and pacing races. Counsilman published the results of his work in *The Science of Swimming* (1968). In this text, he based stroke techniques on scientific principles of physics and mechanics. He created further knowledge by modifying strokes for speed and explaining training methods and techniques. Counsilman's techniques were not concerned with how long swimmers could stay afloat but rather with how fast they could propel themselves throughout the water while complying with certain rules agreed upon by international bodies governing competitive swimming. This approach not only inspired the coaching techniques of Counsilman's contemporaries but also induced them to question and expand existing knowledge.

The trial and error method is no longer necessary for developing efficient stroke mechanics and successful training techniques. Today's potential coaches can benefit from the years of research and knowledge developed in this quest for speed. The following materials were chosen by experienced aquatic professionals as those that are most relevant for coaches of seasonal swimmers.

Chapter 2: The Freestyle

Coaching Objectives for the Freestyle

At the conclusion of this chapter, you should understand how to teach the freestyle to beginning swimmers. This chapter presents the following:

- Helpful terms referring to the freestyle.
- Body position, armstroke, kick, and breathing for the freestyle.
- Coaching points to be emphasized in the freestyle.
- Drills for learning and developing the freestyle.
- Starts and turns appropriate for the freestyle.
- Coaching points to be emphasized in freestyle starts and turns.

Helpful Terms

Freestyle. A swimming style in which any stroke may be used. In competitive swimming, freestyle is synonymous with the front crawl.
Recovery arm. The arm that is preparing to take another stroke.
Stroking arm. The arm that moves underwater to propel the swimmer through the water.
Flutter kick. The alternating up-and-down leg movement used in the freestyle.
Streamlined position. The efficient, fully extended position taken by a swimmer to move through the water following a start or turn.
"T." The point at which the stripe on the bottom of the pool, parallel to the turning wall, crosses the swimming lane line, forming a "T" and signaling the turn.
Long axis. The imaginary line running vertically through the body from the head to the toes.

Body Position

Check your freestylers to ensure that they are in a prone body position nearly horizontal to the surface of the water. The water should cut the head approximately at the hairline with the hips and legs maintained just below the surface. Tell your swimmers that as they start to pull, the body will roll evenly on the long axis toward the forward arm. The arms then attain maximum efficiency and easy recovery because of reduced frontal resistance (see Figure 2-1).

Fig. 2-1

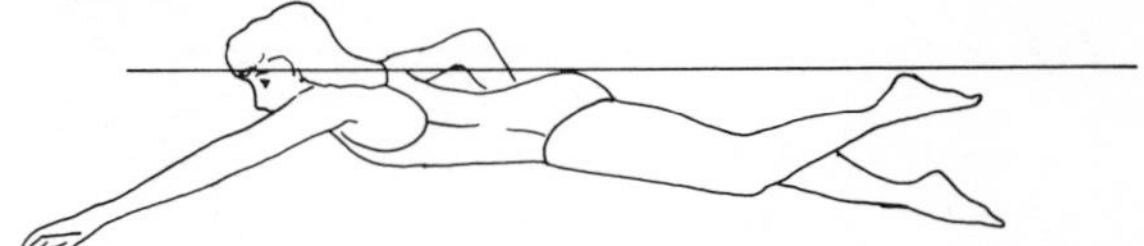

Armstroke

A proper armstroke requires complete concentration, so have your swimmers try it first on land and then in the prone body position in the water without breathing or kicking. Start your explanation with the recovery phase. At the beginning of the recovery, the elbow swings forward, breaking the water, and the bend in the elbow increases. The elbow is carried high as the hand clears the water but stays near the surface (see Figure 2-2). The drills on pages 12-13 are useful for teaching the armstroke.

Fig. 2-2

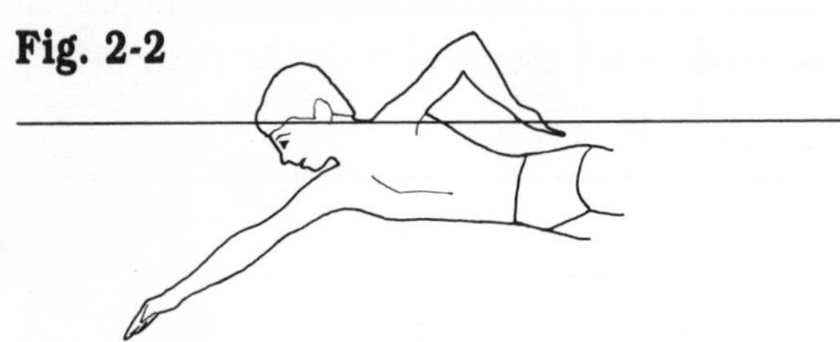

As the arm reaches forward, the hand is pitched at a 45-degree angle with the palm turned outward. The arm becomes the stroking arm when the hand enters the water, fingertips leading, and the elbow extends to return to an almost straight position (see Figure 2-3).

Fig. 2-3

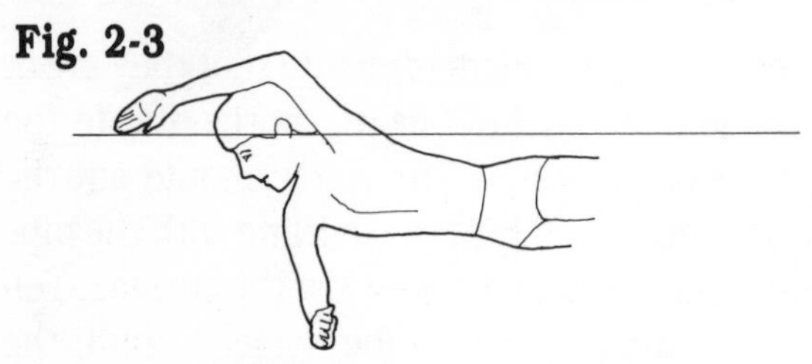

The forearm then rotates, causing the thumb to come up and the fingers to point across the body. Constant water pressure should be felt on the palm of the hand (see Figure 2-4).

Fig. 2-4

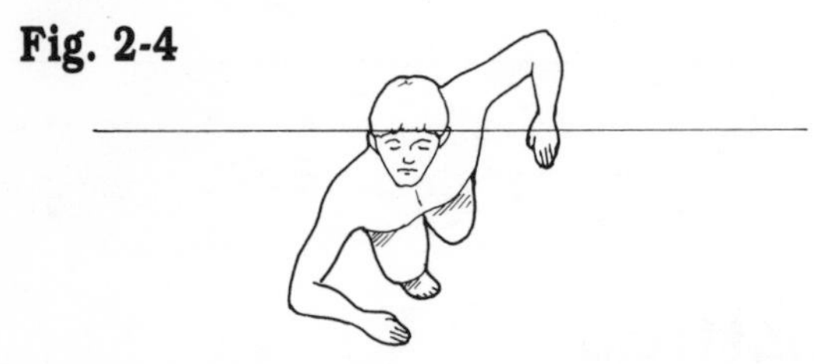

Next, the fingers of the stroking arm are pointed at the bottom of the pool. The arm is not quite extended as the hand continues to a point below the bottom of the bathing suit to begin the recovery phase of the stroke (see Figure 2-5).

If looked at from the bottom of the pool, each hand would be making an "S" as it pulls back under the body (see Figure 2-6).

Fig. 2-5

Fig. 2-6

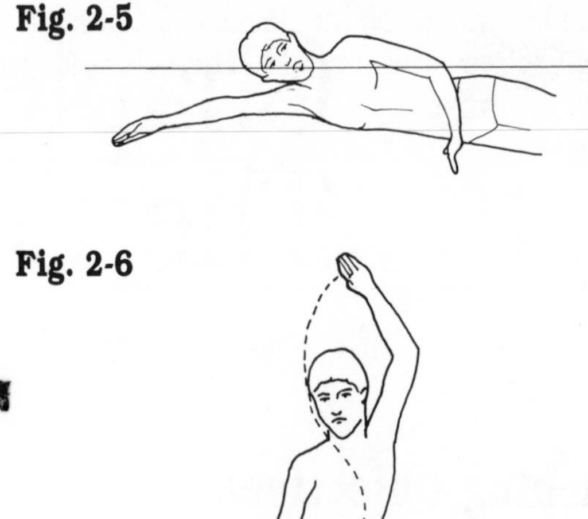

Coaching Points for the Freestyle Armstroke

1. Elbow should be high on the recovery.
2. Fingertips should enter the water first.
3. Elbow should be high during the pull.
4. Constant water pressure should be felt on the stroking hand.
5. Stroking arm should be pushed past the bathing suit.

The Flutter Kick

The flutter kick, a term that does not truly describe the freestyle leg action, is an alternating up-and-down movement of the legs. To perfect the flutter kick, have your swimmers hang on to a wall with both hands with their legs extended in back of them (see Figure 2-7).

Have the swimmers start the kicking movement from the hips. As the thigh moves down, the knee bends slightly due to the resistance of the water. At the bottom of the kick, the leg

Fig. 2-7

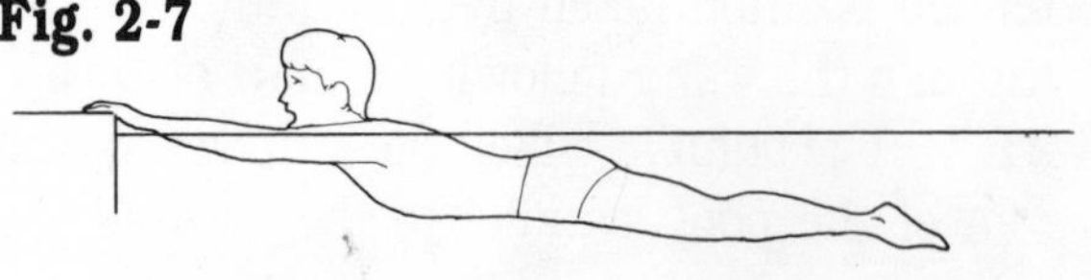

should be straight but not locked. When the leg starts back up, it is straight. Then, in reaction to momentum, it bends slightly at the knee joint as the kick is completed (See Figures 2-8 to 2-10.).

Fig. 2-8

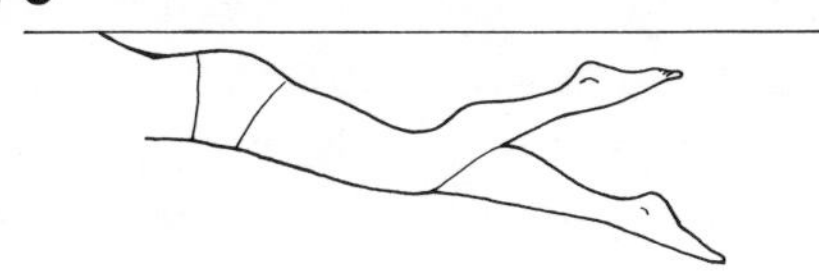

Fig. 2-9

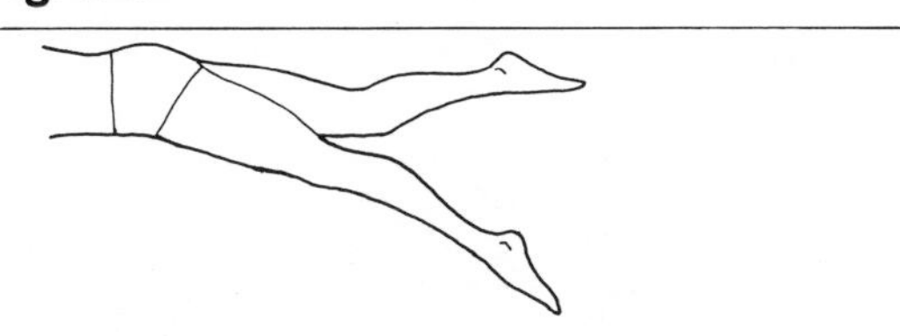

Fig. 2-10

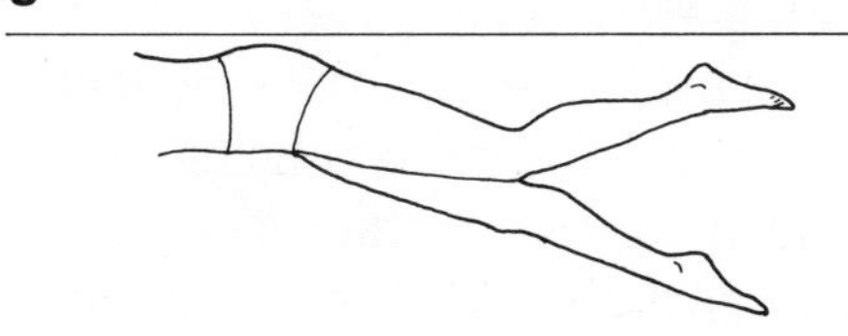

Emphasize to your swimmers that only the heels should break the surface of the water. The width of the kick, or separation of the feet, is 8 to 16 inches depending on the length of the legs. A loose ankle that flicks at the end of the kick is common to the most efficient kick, and a toeing in of the feet results when the ankle is relaxed enough to give the flicking motion.

Your swimmers are kicking correctly when the water at their feet looks and sounds like it is boiling. Tell your swimmers to listen to their kicks. If they hear a sharp splash at the feet, the knees are bent too much; if there is no sound at the feet, there is insufficient kick. When swimmers can do the kick correctly, they are ready to progress to the drills on pages 12-13.

The main purpose of the freestyle leg action is body balance, not propulsion. Encourage your swimmers to develop a cadence of six beats to a stroke because this kick is most often used in the shorter distances. Many swimmers automatically go into a two-beat crossover kick for distances. In the two-beat kick, the leg thrusts downward as the arm on the same side thrusts upward. When observed from the rear, the legs can be seen to cross. This kick is never taught. If swimmers develop it naturally, however, they should be allowed to use it.

Coaching Points for the Flutter Kick

1. Kick from the hips.
2. Legs should be straight but not locked.
3. Ankles should be loose, resulting in a slight toeing in of the feet.
4. Water at the heels should look like it is boiling.

The Freestyle Breathing Pattern

Swimmers choose their own breathing side by deciding what feels best or most natural to them. Inhalation occurs through the mouth when the hand on the breathing side is at the end of its pull. This coordinates the breath with the normal roll of the body so that swimmers inhale when the mouth is at the bottom of a trough created by the body's forward motion. Exhalation occurs through the nose and mouth as the head is turned back into the water. Swimmers breathe constantly either in or out when practicing the freestyle.

A swimmer having trouble with the breathing pattern should practice it with the feet on the bottom of the pool and the body bent over so that the upper body is in a swimming position. Be sure that the swimmer keeps the ear in the water while turning to breathe (see Figure 2-11) and returns the head to center after each breath. Check the armstroke and kicking drills for other ways to practice breathing.

Fig. 2-11

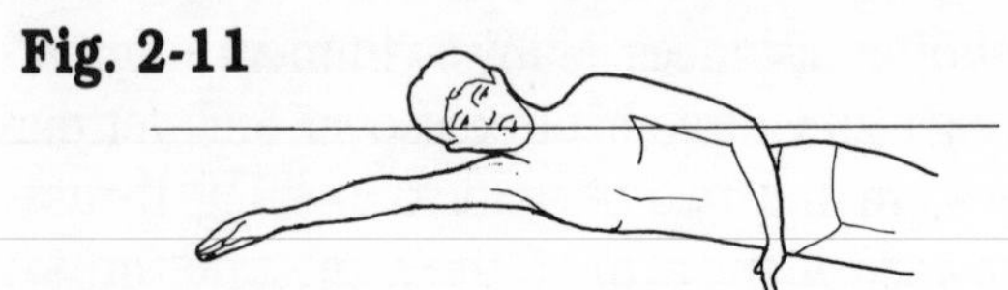

Coaching Points for the Freestyle Breathing Pattern

1. Inhale as the arm on the breathing side is at the end of the pull.
2. Inhale through the mouth.
3. Exhale through the nose and mouth.
4. Breathe constantly either in or out.

Drills for Practicing the Freestyle

The following freestyle drills will help your swimmers develop the kicking and armstroking techniques described in this chapter. Additionally, hypoxic or restrictive breathing drills are suggested that can aid each swimmer's efficiency.

Flutter Kicking Drills

(2.1) Kick Board Under Armpits
The flutter kick, breaststroke kick, or butterfly kick is practiced with the swimmers' heads above water so that they can hear the coach's instructions (see Figure 2-12).

Fig. 2-12

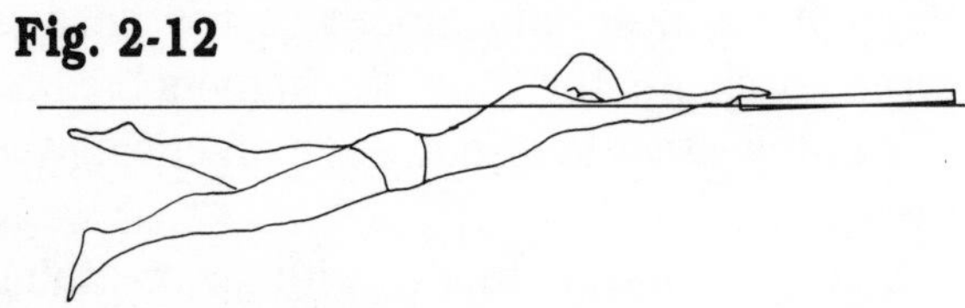

(2.2) Kick Board Extended
The swimmer holds the board by the near edge with the arms extended. This method allows the swimmer to practice breathing and eliminates socializing during kicking drills. It also puts the body in the swimming position (see Figure 2-13).

Fig. 2-13

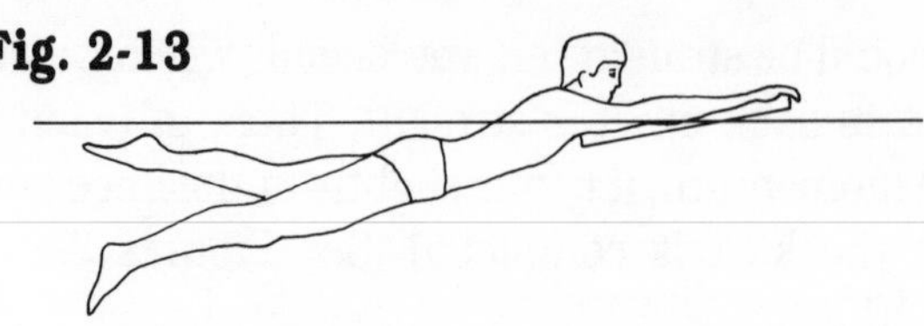

(2.3) Kicking Without a Board
This drill is done with swimmers lying on their sides. The arm closer to the bottom of the pool is extended straight in front of the swimmer's head. The other arm rests by the side. This drill develops a relaxed, flexible kick (see Figure 2-14).

Fig. 2-14

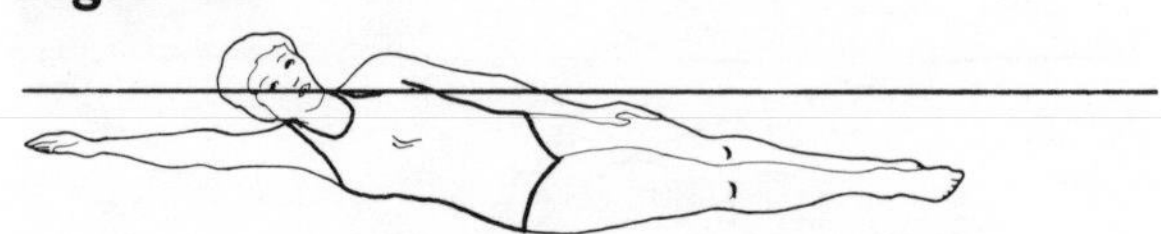

Armstroke and Breathing Drills

(2.4) Pulling With a Kickboard
The board is held in front of the swimmer with both arms extended. One arm holds the board while the arm on the breathing side pulls with the "S" pattern armstroke. The breath should be taken as the pull nears completion. Emphasize to the swimmers not to recover the arm until the inhalation has been made and the head is ready to roll back. Tell the swimmers that when the first armstroke is completed, they should hold the board with the first arm and pull with the other arm. This drill perfects the timing of the breathing as well as the mechanics of the stroke.

(2.5) Pulling With One Arm
Using a six-beat kick, the swimmers progress down the pool using only one arm. The other arm stays straight in front of the head, acting as a rudder. The arms reverse rolls when swimming back. This drill perfects the "S" pattern of the stroke.

(2.6) Duck Drill
Thumbs are hooked under the armpits. Using the kick, breathing pattern, and adjusted armstroke, the swimmers make their way down the

pool. This drill emphasizes the high elbow of the recovery.

(2.7) Advanced Duck Drill
Swimmers use the regular freestyle but draw the thumb up beside the body, touching it to the armpit on each recovery. This drill is used to eliminate the straight arm recovery common to swimmers who learned that the freestyle should be swum with a windmill movement.

Hypoxic Drills

The term *hypoxic* applies to inhaling less air by restricting breathing, thus making less oxygen available to the cells. The hypoxic drill is used only with swimmers with proficient breathing skills. It should not be used with beginning swimmers. For this drill, the swimmer is given a slower than normal breathing pattern that limits oxygen intake. For example, the coach tells a swimmer to make a regulated number of strokes between breaths or to take a regulated number of breaths per length. Studies have shown that swimmers can benefit from controlled breathing, and many college swimming programs have used hypoxic training consistently and beneficially since these studies. This training technique can be adapted to your programs if the following guidelines are followed:

- Keep in mind that unconsciousness can result if the breath is held too long. Be alert!
- If swimmers develop headaches, decrease the use of hypoxic drills.
- No more than one fourth of the total workout should be done hypoxically.
- The shorter the distance to be swum, the more strokes may be taken between breaths.
- The hypoxic technique should not be used in competition.
- Swimmers must be reminded to maintain good stroke mechanics while using hypoxic drills.
- Never attempt to see how far swimmers can go without breathing.

(2.8) 5 × 100 Yards With 1-Minute Rest
Have your swimmers swim 100 yards five times with a 1-minute rest between each 100 yards. Tell the swimmers to breathe six times on the first length of 100 yards, five times on the second length, four times on the third length and three times on the fourth length.

(2.9) 10 × 50 Yards on 1-Minute
Have your swimmers swim 50 yards ten times, swimming one 50-yard length and then resting for the duration of each minute. Tell your swimmers to breathe regularly on the first length and to breathe every fifth stroke on the second length of each set. Do not conduct this set hypoxically until your swimmers can accomplish it easily without restricted breathing.

(2.10) 1 × 300-Yard Crawl
Have your swimmers swim 300 yards. The first two lengths are done slowly. The third length is done fast with only five breaths for the length. Repeat the cycle four times in a 25-yard pool.

Freestyle Starts

In a race, the swimmer is moving faster coming off the wall after a turn or coming out of a dive than at any other point in the race. Therefore, time spent teaching swimmers how to take advantage of this tremendous momentum through proper pull-outs and streamlining of their bodies during the glide phases of these techniques is very productive.

Teach all starts in deep water without starting blocks. When you know that your swimmers can control their entries, you can begin to have them try starts from the blocks.

The Grab Start

First teach your swimmers the starting position. Explain that on the command, *Take your mark*, the swimmers bend over and grab the blocks or pool deck with their feet under their hips and their hands inside their feet. The toes are curled over the edge, and the weight is distributed over the balls of the feet to provide balance. The chin is tucked so that the eyes look between the knees, not toward you (see Figure 2-15).

Fig. 2-15

A demonstration will show that on the command *Go*, the swimmers pull forward against the blocks. As they lose their balance forward, the head is lifted and the arms swing directly forward. A push through the hips, knees, and ankles extends the body. The arms should be in front of the body with the hands below eye level and angled toward the water (see Figure 2-16).

Fig. 2-16

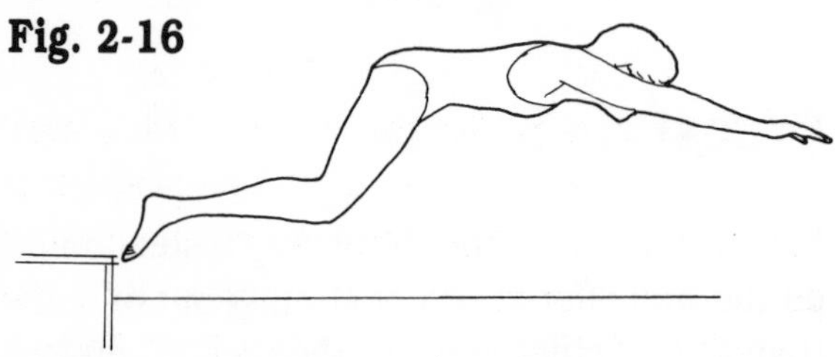

At full extension, the head drops slightly, and the hands, placed one on top of the other, hit the water first as the head drop continues (see Figure 2-17).

Fig. 2-17

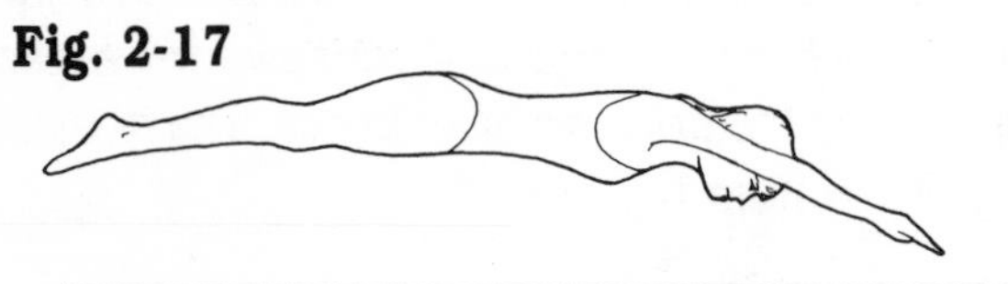

After your demonstration, have the swimmers try the dive entering the water as if diving into a hole and then streamlining the body by stretching hard with the extended arms placed directly over the ears. The hands are still together, one on top of the other, as a few quick kicks drive the swimmer to the surface. When the momentum from the dive ends, the armstroke begins. Because even a slight turn of the head will break the streamlined position that affords maximum momentum, the start is not finished until the swimmers have taken three strokes without a breath.

The Relay Start

Swimming relays provide an opportunity for teammates to swim one after another in a combined effort. The rules permit the second, third, and fourth swimmers to start their dives before the incoming teammate has finished the previous segment of the race. However, some part of the body must be in contact with the starting blocks until the preceding teammate touches the finish. Therefore, to promote the best relay starts for your team, have swimmers practice a recoiling circular arm movement timed to the finish of the previous swimmer. This gets the take-off swimmer further away from the wall than the grab start. Because timing is vital, warn incoming relay swimmers to maintain their stroke length and turnover rate at the finish.

To teach this skill to your team, have the swimmers stand with feet apart with body weight and arms forward as shown in Figure 2-18.

Fig. 2-18

Each swimmer then drops the head and brings the arms upward and back as the incoming swimmer's arm is in the final recovery. The diver's arms continue around, the knees bend, and the heels lift off the block as shown in Figure 2-19.

Fig. 2-19

The head lifts as the forward circling arms and the legs thrust the swimmer's body to full extension. Contact with the block is maintained until the incoming swimmer hits the finish. The arms stop as they reach a position diagonal to the water (see Figure 2-20).

Fig. 2-20

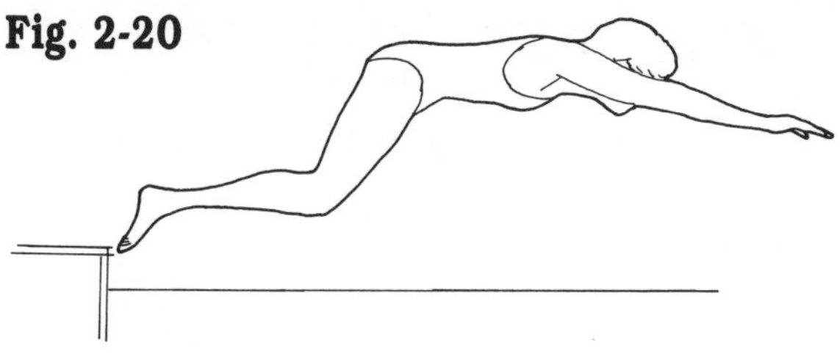

As in the grab start, the head drops between the arms, causing the hands to enter the water first. Again, the swimmer streamlines, kicks to the surface, and takes three strokes before assuming a normal breathing pattern (see Figure 2-21).

Fig. 2-21

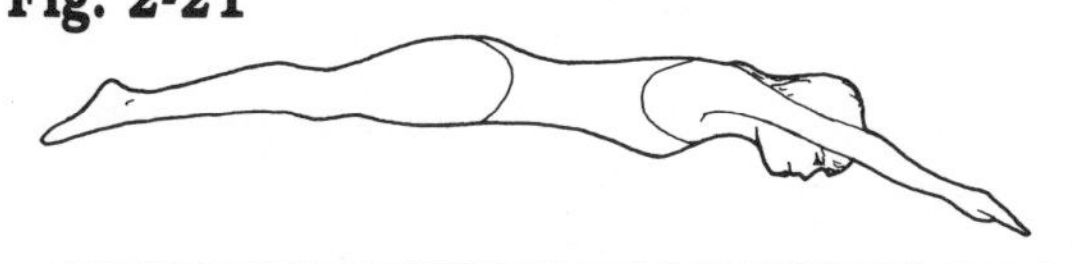

Your swimmers have accomplished this technique when they can time their start to the finish of the incoming swimmer.

Freestyle Flip Turn

Your freestyle swimmers must learn to change direction efficiently and legally; that is some part of the swimmer's body must contact the end wall. Swimmers learn the turn in three parts: the approach to the wall, the flip, and the push-off from the wall.

Push-Off from the Wall

Teach the push-off from a wall first. Ask your swimmers to sink underwater and place both feet on the wall. The feet should be parallel to the bottom, 6 to 10 inches below the water surface. The swimmer pushes off on the side and then turns onto the abdomen as the body is extended (see Figure 2-22). One hand is on top of the other,

Fig. 2-22

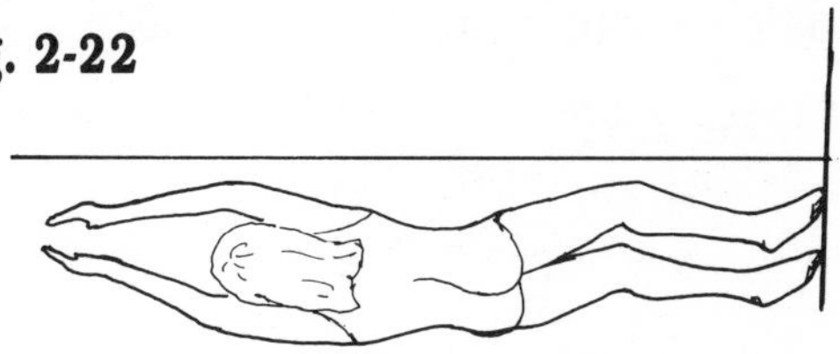

and you should emphasize the need for a hard stretch right through the toes. The position is held until the swimmer slows to swimming speed and then the kick starts, followed by the arms with the bottom arm stroking first. At least three strokes should be taken before the swimmer breathes.

The Flip

Next teach the flip portion of the turn. Have the competitors try flips, gaining momentum by pushing off the bottom of the pool as shown in Figure 2-23.

Fig. 2-23

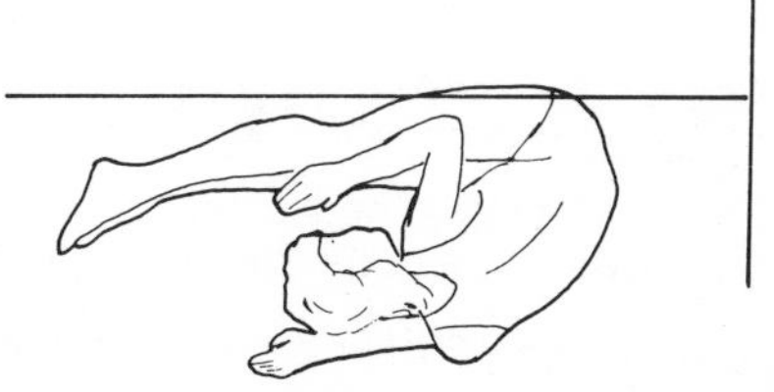

If the swimmer has trouble learning the flip, use the following partner system:

- The learner floats with the hands at the sides. The partner holds the learner's near hand with the hand closer to the swimmer's feet as shown in Figure 2-24.

Fig. 2-24

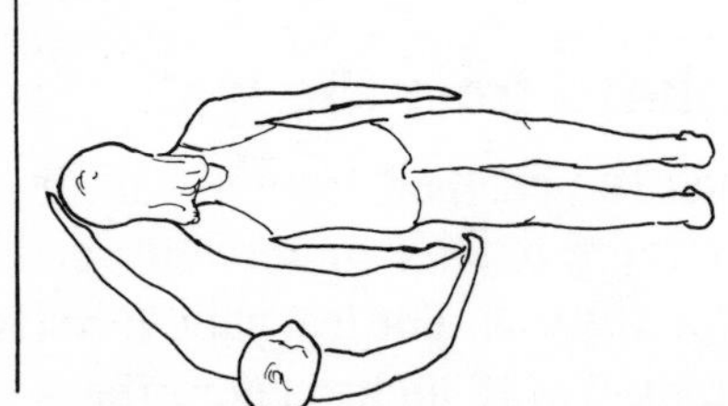

- The partner's other hand presses the learner's head to the knees and lets the learner's legs come straight over (see Figure 2-25).

Fig. 2-25

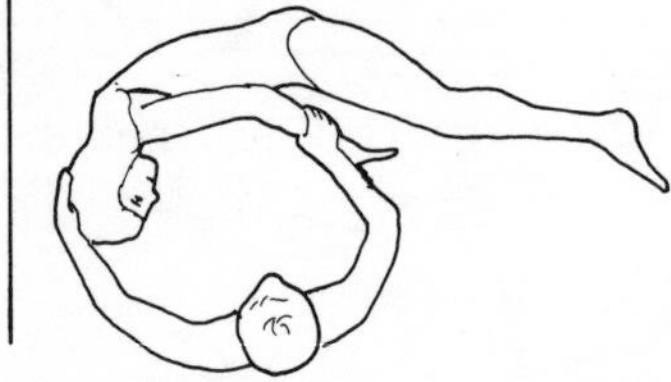

- The partner repeats the action close to a wall. This time, have the swimmer drag the free arm across the body so that the swimmer will twist and flip. The partner can then drop the hand to assist the swimmer's feet as they hit the wall (see Figure 2-26).

Fig. 2-26

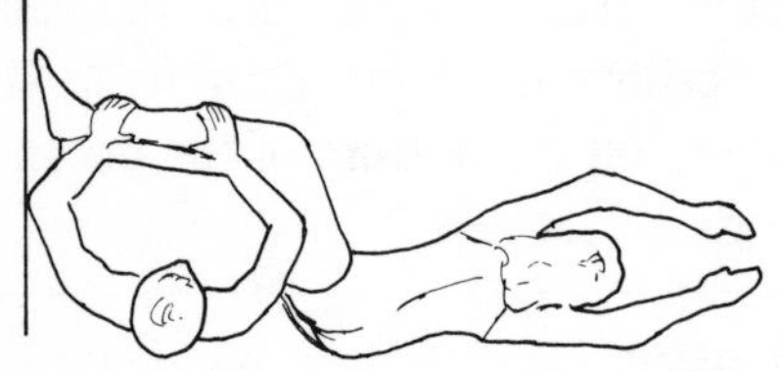

- Now have the swimmers try the motion without partners.

When swimmers can do the twist and flip, they swim into the wall and do the half flip combined with the one-quarter twist as they practiced with their partners. After they flip, the streamlined position is taken as they push off on their sides.

The Approach to the Turn

Now teach the approach to the turn. The approach is taught over lane lines so that the swimmers can see how many strokes they must take after crossing the "T" before they start to flip. Tell the swimmers to approach the wall with a normal stroke. The arm completing the push of the stroke pauses at the hip and drags across the body to help start the turn (see Figure 2-27).

Fig. 2-27

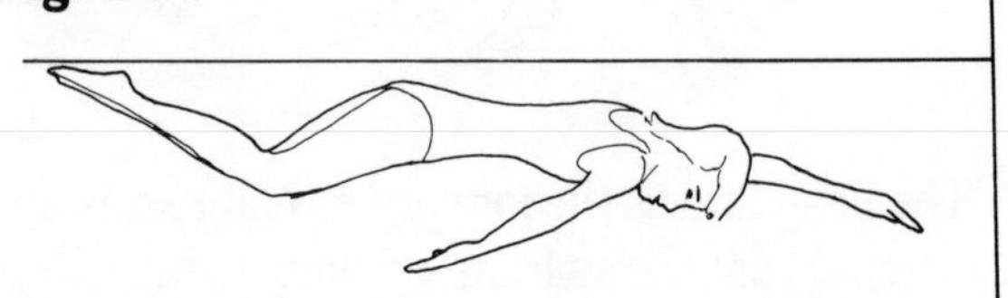

The other arm continues to pull as the head drops and the feet give a hard kick to help drive the hips upward and the feet over the water. Proper distance from the wall is achieved if the knees are only partially bent when the foot contacts the wall (see Figure 2-28).

Fig. 2-28

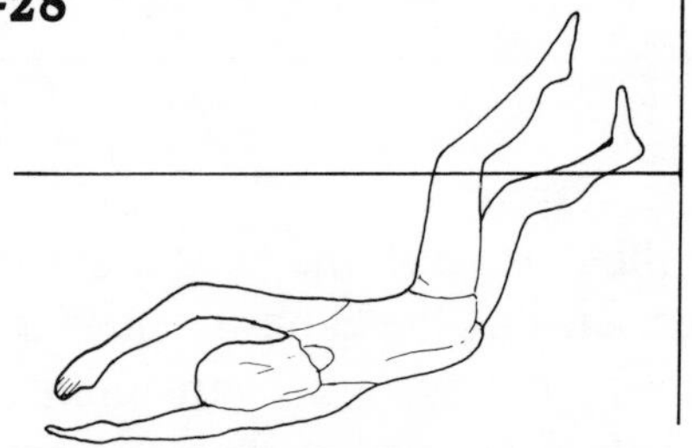

Coaching Points for the Flip Turn

1. Both hands should provide the momentum for the flip.
2. The turn is a half somersault with a one-quarter twist.
3. The legs should be tucked only as far as they would be if the swimmer were going to take a vertical jump on land.

4. Streamline after every turn, even in practice.
5. Take three strokes after each turn before breathing.
6. Consider turns a chance to gain time, not to stop and rest.

Evaluating Your Progress

1. Choose the diagram demonstrating the correct head position. _____

Fig. 2-29

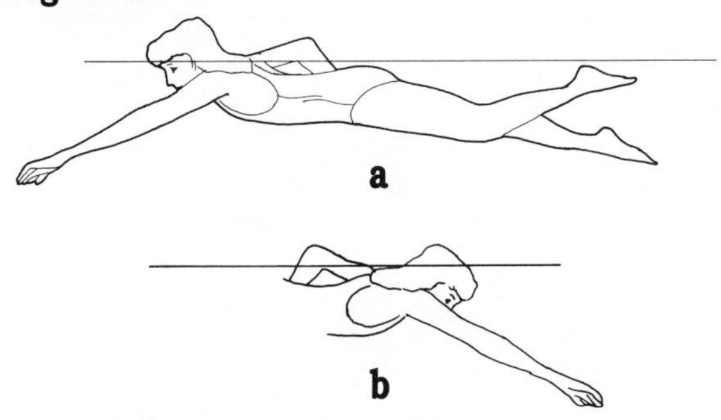

2. Choose the diagram demonstrating the correct inhalation phase of the breathing. _____

Fig. 2-30

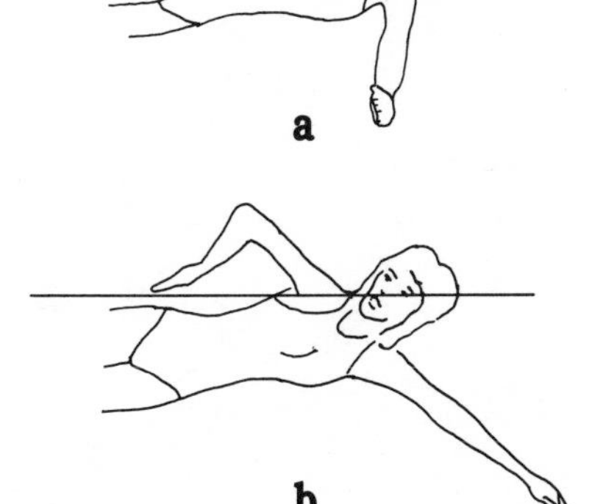

3. What key words would you use with a swimmer who is
   a. using a straight arm recovery?
   b. holding the head out of water too long on the inhalation?
   c. kicking with the knees bent?
4. How would you best describe the hand entry position?
   a. Little finger side of hand enters first.
   b. Palm is turned outward with the fingertips leading.
   c. Palm faces straight back with the fingertips leading.
5. Which starting situation requires swimmers to steady themselves by grabbing the starting block?
   a. Starting on a relay
   b. Starting on a command
6. Where is the body weight when a swimmer assumes the starting position?
   a. Over the balls of the feet
   b. Back on the heels
   c. Over the toes
7. How should the swimmer enter the water from the start?
   a. As if diving into a hole
   b. Flat on the surface of the water
8. What is the correct position of the body when pushing off following the crawl flip turn?
   a. Extended on the side
   b. Extended facedown
9. Which diagram correctly illustrates the legs being brought over the water to the wall in the flip turn?

Fig. 2-31

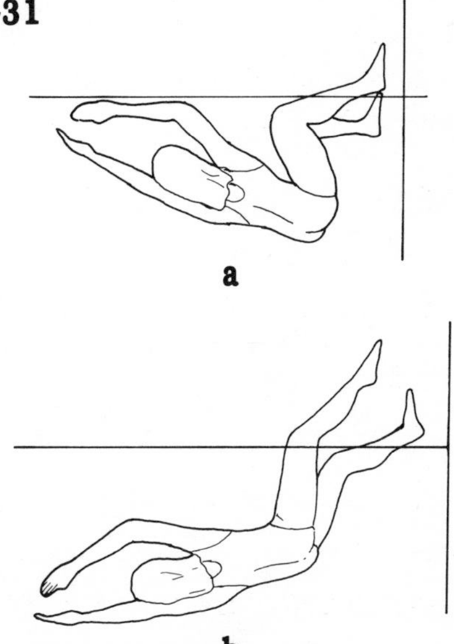

Chapter 3: The Backstroke

Coaching Objectives for the Backstroke

At the conclusion of this chapter, you should understand how to effectively teach the backstroke to beginning swimmers. This chapter presents the following:

- Helpful terms referring to the backstroke.
- Body position, armstroke, kick, and breathing for the backstroke.
- Coaching points to be emphasized in the backstroke.
- Drills for learning and developing the backstroke.
- Start and turn appropriate for the backstroke.
- Coaching points to be emphasized in the backstroke start and turn.

Helpful Terms

Natural buoyancy. A swimmer's innate ability to stay afloat.
Long axis. The imaginary line running vertically through the body from the head to the toes on which the body rotates when swimming the backstroke.
Backstroke flip turn. At least three backstroke turns are commonly used. However, the easiest to perform legally and efficiently is termed the *flip turn.*
Recovery arm. The arm that is preparing for another propulsive stroke.
Stroking arm. The arm involved in the propulsive action.
Backstroke flags. Equipment placed 7 feet above the water and 15 feet from the wall to warn backstrokers of approaching turns.

Body Position

Your backstroke swimmers should be streamlined and extended on the back with the hips no more than 6 to 8 inches below the surface of the water. This hip position is determined largely by the placement of the head, the effectiveness of the kick, and the swimmer's natural buoyancy. Swimmers should know that they should not stay flat on their backs in swimming the backstroke. Instead, the head remains still while the body rotates 45 degrees on the long axis toward the stroking arm side. This body roll allows the recovering arm and shoulder to move forward without creating excessive drag (see Figure 3-1).

Fig. 3-1

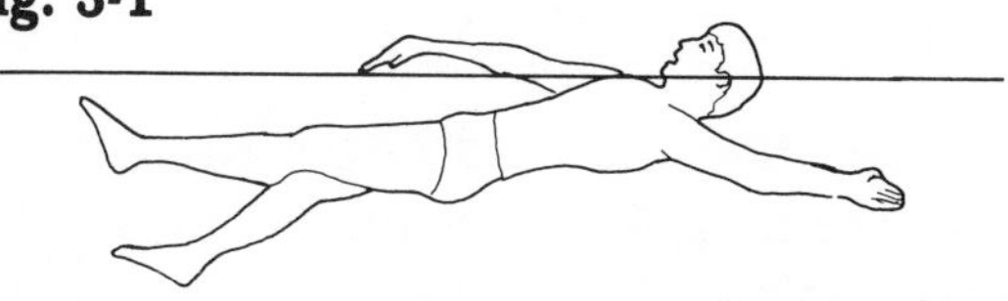

Work with each swimmer individually to teach the proper stationary head position. A line from the ears to the eyes should be 45 degrees off the water with the head in the water to ear level. When correcting the body position, note that if the head is tilted too far back, the hips will rise too high (see Figure 3-2). If the chin is down, the hips will drop to a sitting position and the body will not be streamlined.

Fig. 3-2

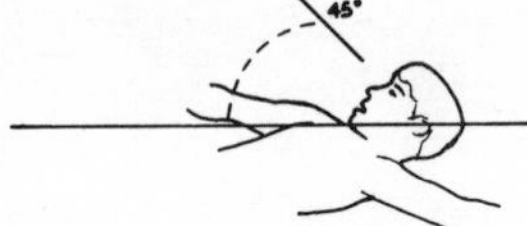

Backstroke Arm Motion

Swimmers work the arms in opposition. One straight arm enters the water at a point directly over the shoulder as the opposite arm starts to recover, as shown in Figure 3-3.

Fig. 3-3

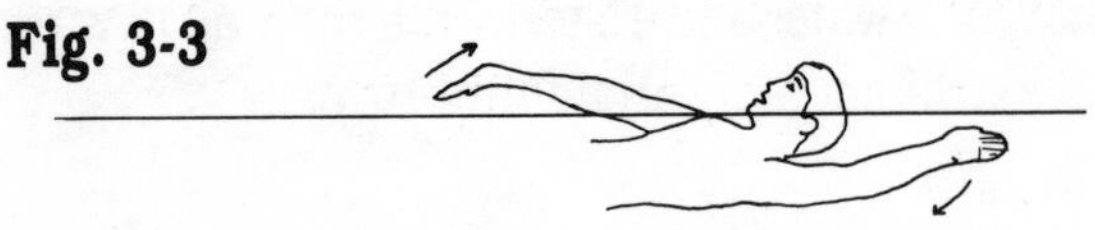

The backstroker's hand enters the water 12 inches from the midline of the body. Have your swimmers compare their arm entry positions to the points of 11:00 and 1:00 on the face of a clock (see Figure 3-4).

Fig. 3-4

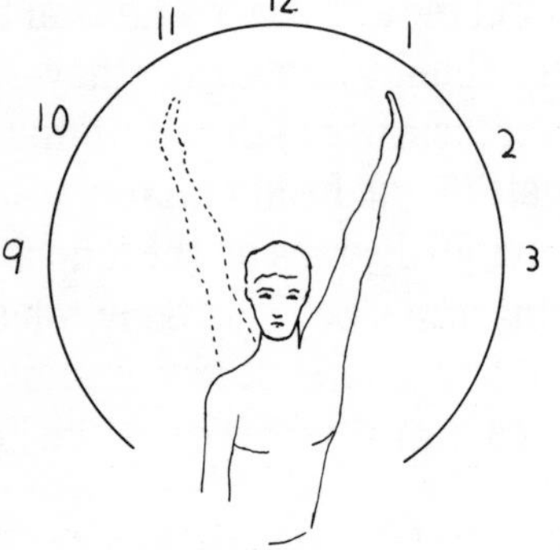

Explain that the hand of the stroking arm should be at a 90-degree angle with the little finger leading. This hand sinks downward 8 to 12 inches as the pull begins and the body rolls toward this lead arm. The swimmer then presses the hand outward and toward the feet. The elbow bends to a 90-degree angle, allowing the entire forearm to engage in the push of water toward the feet. The swimmer's stroking arm now becomes the recovery arm. It leaves the water in a relaxed position and moves directly upward and forward in the vertical plane back to the point of entry (see Figure 3-5).

Fig. 3-5

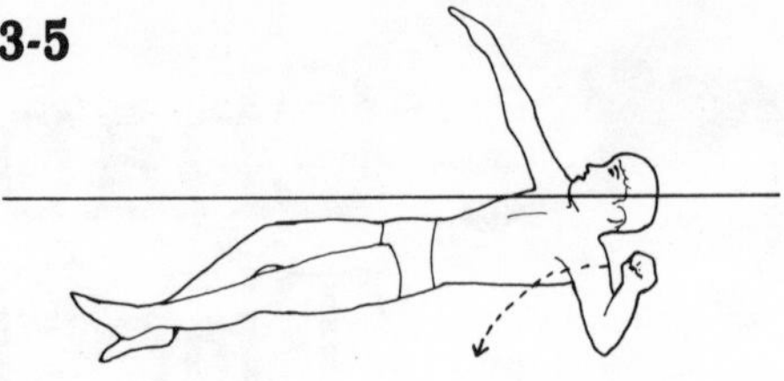

Ensure that the elbow of the swimmer's pulling arm extends at the end of the motion and that the hand pushes to a point just below the buttocks, completing an "S" pattern. (see Figure 3-6). Only then do the shoulders return to the horizontal plane and the hand prepares to recover.

Fig. 3-6

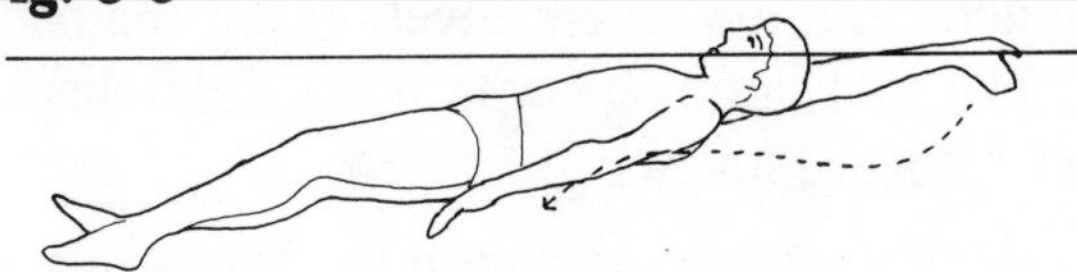

Coaching Points for the Armstroke

1. Arms should move continuously and in opposition.
2. Little finger should lead in the entry.
3. Hands should enter at 11:00 and 1:00 o'clock positions on the face of a clock.
4. Elbows should be at a 90-degree angle on the pull.

Backstroke Kick and Breathing Pattern

Your swimmers should use a six-beat flutter kick with each backstroke arm cycle. This can be demonstrated on land in a sitting position. The legs and feet should be relaxed. On the downbeat, the legs are straight; on the upbeat, the knees bend slightly. When done in the water, only the big toe of each foot should be seen causing the water to churn at the feet. The depth of the up-and-down movement of the kick is approximately the same as the width of the swimmer's shoulders. Explain that breathing is continuous and should be synchronized to the arm movement by inhaling on the recovery of the alternate arm.

Coaching Points for the Backstroke

1. Six kicks should be made with each arm cycle.
2. Legs should be almost straight.
3. Only the big toe should break the water.
4. Synchronize breathing to the recovery of the alternate arm.

Drills for Practicing the Backstroke

(3.1) Dry Land Drill
One swimmer lies on the back on a bench on dry land. Move the swimmer's arm through the "S" pattern to give the swimmer the feel of the movement and allow teammates to visualize the process. If a swimmer in the water is pulling incorrectly, do not hesitate to have the swimmer leave the pool and practice the stroke in this manner.

(3.2) Shallow Water Drill
Have your swimmers stand in armpit-depth water. One arm reaches back, entering the water with the little finger leading. This arm makes the "S" pattern with the hand, emphasizing the press down at the end of the stroke. The swimmer then tries the drill with the other hand. The first time the drill is done, allow the swimmer to turn the head and watch the hand. When the motion is grooved, the head is held stationary during the drill. Finally, the swimmer does the drill with alternate arms.

(3.3) Double Arm Backstroke Drill
A regular flutter kick is used as both arms are brought over the top of the water simultaneously. This drill is easier than trying to move the arms in opposition. The drill also develops shoulder joint flexibility.

(3.4) One Arm Backstroke Drill
One arm is in the water over the head. It acts as a rudder while the other arm performs the pull. Arms are reversed at the end of each length. A variation of the drill places the arm not in use by the hip. More body roll is allowed when the drill is performed in this position.

(3.5) Head Position Drill
You stand on a block or diving board at the end of the pool. From this position, you hold up diving score cards or lap counters. The backstrokers keep their eyes on the numbers in order to know the ones that have been flashed. To ensure that your swimmers keep their heads at a 45-degree angle, raise the numbers as they get farther away. At the end of the length, ask the swimmers to recall the numbers. This drill demands a stationary head position with the eyes 45 degrees off the water.

Backstroke Start

At the starting block end of the pool, demonstrate how to grasp the block with the hands slightly outside the shoulders. The feet are positioned on a gutter or against the wall. Then show the swimmers that at the command *Take your mark*, they are to pull themselves close to the block by flexing the elbows downward and bringing the knees between them (see Figure 3-7).

Fig. 3-7

On the command *Go*, the head is snapped back and the hands sweep backward and upward to the side as shown in Figure 3-8.

Fig. 3-8

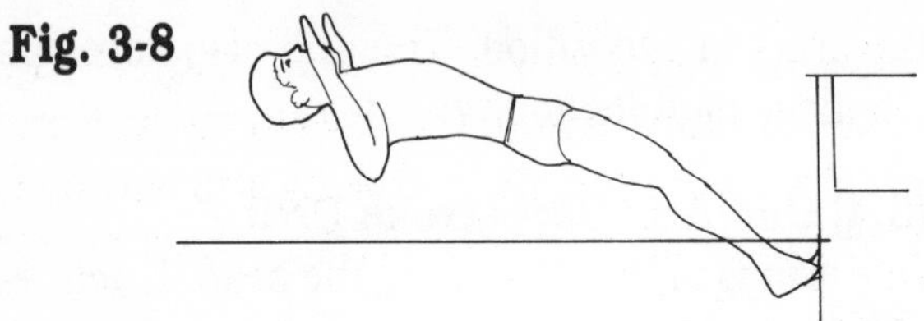

Now the starting swimmer brings the hands to an extended position over the head, and the hips are lifted clear of the water (see Figure 3-9).

Fig. 3-9

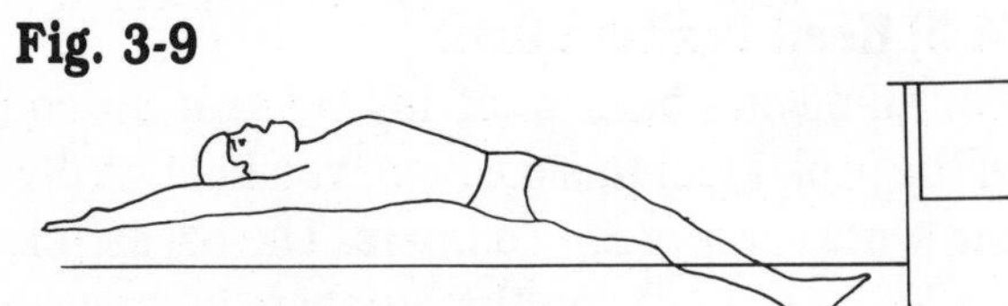

The extended position is maintained as the fingertips enter the water first, as shown in Figure 3-10.

Fig. 3-10

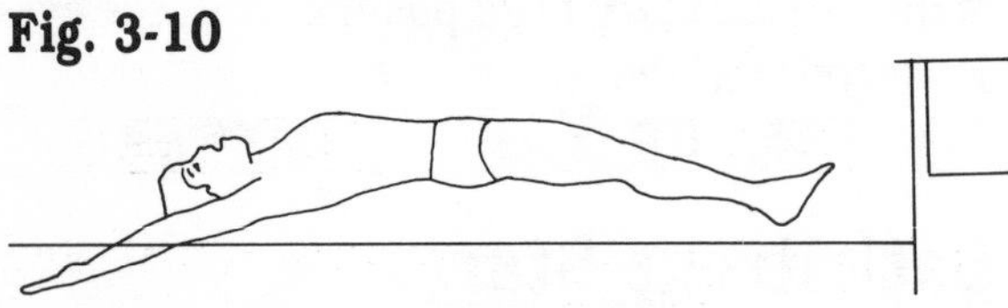

A kicking motion begins as soon as the momentum of the glide is lost. One arm pulls to the surface, the eyes are set on a target 45 degrees off the water, and the armstroke continues.

Backstroke Turn

Swimmers approaching the wall for the backstroke turn must remain on their backs. Swimming rules state that the backstroker's shoulders must not turn over beyond the vertical plane until the foremost hand touches the wall. A competitor who continuously looks at the wall when approaching a turn loses time, breaks the streamlined position of the body, and risks a disqualification. However, the distance from the flags to the turning wall may vary from pool to pool. Although you want your backstrokers to keep their heads in a stationary position, allow them to take one look when approaching a turn. This can be done if swimmers are trained to count their strokes from the flags to the turning wall during practice, so have your flags in place at all times.

The Pivot Position

Teach the pivot position first. The pivot portion of the turn can be taught on dry land against a wall. Demonstrate that the extended hand touches low with the elbow bent and the fingers pointing toward the opposite shoulder. The swimmers turn and roll onto the upper back as the legs are brought upward toward the hand that hit while the head moves to the open side. The feet touch the wall where the hand was. Have your swimmers practice this movement on land and be sure that they wear a sweatshirt for protection.

Next, try this in the water. Ensure that the swimmer's forward hand touches the turning wall 8 to 12 inches below the surface of the water. Again, the fingers of the touching hand point toward the opposite shoulder (see Figure 3-11).

Fig. 3-11

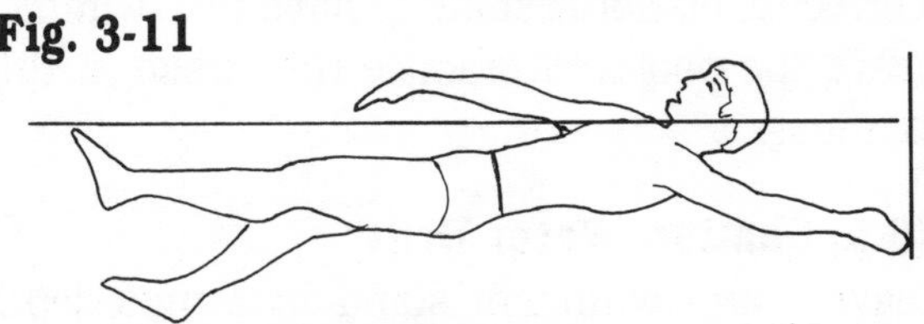

The kick continues until the elbow of the touching hand is bent. Then the knees are squeezed together, and the head and shoulders are submerged as they move away from the hand that hit (see Figure 3-12).

With the aid of the free hand, moving in a reverse sculling motion toward the head, the knees are thrown over the surface of the water toward the hand that hit the wall. Swimmers that have done the freestyle flip turn should be able to grasp the concept of a half back somersault. As they do this, they should end up plac-

Fig. 3-12

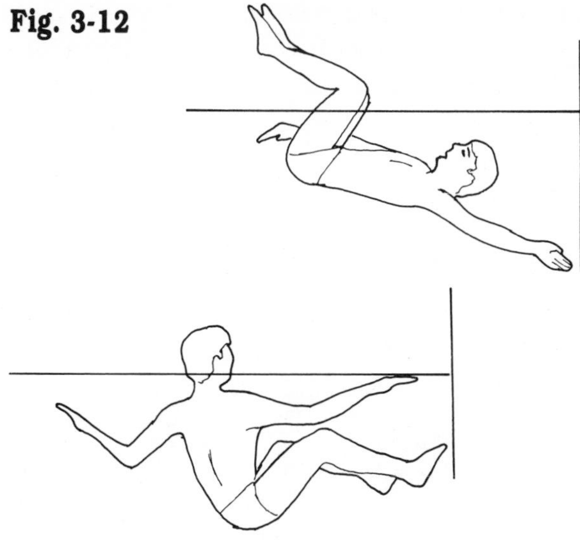

ing the feet on the wall where the hand touched (see Figure 3-13).

Fig. 3-13

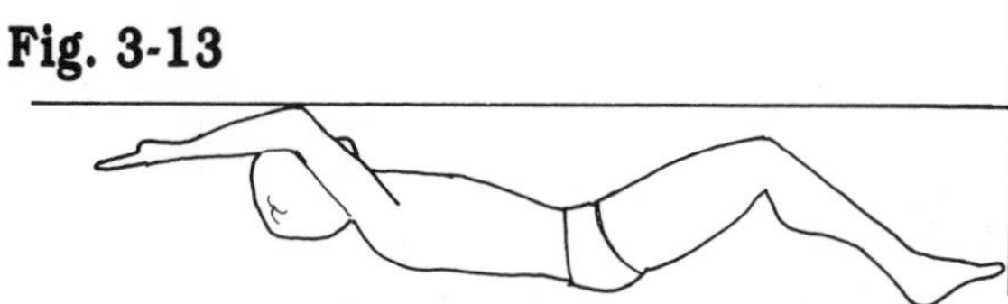

The Push-Off

Next teach the streamlined push-off with the swimmers on their backs in the water. Swimmers should experiment to find a spot 8 to 12 inches below the water surface for their feet. They should be able to push off efficiently from this spot. The hands are placed one on top of the other as in a face-down streamlined position. Be sure to emphasize stretching out with the arms and positioning the head between them as the swimmer leaves the wall (see Figure 3-14).

Fig. 3-14

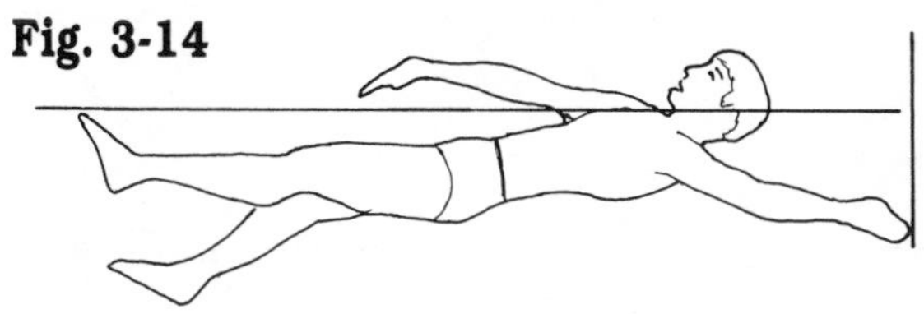

The Approach to the Turn

Now teach the approach to the turn. Swimmers should start three or four strokes beyond the flags. As they swim to the wall, they should count the strokes from the flags to the wall and look backward over their stroking arm only once before touching the wall and trying the complete turn.

Coaching Points for the Backstroke Turn

1. Head should be in a stationary position when approaching the turn.
2. Lead hand should touch the wall 8 to 12 inches below the water surface.
3. Elbow of the lead arm should be bent.
4. Head should move away from the hand that hit.
5. Feet should hit the wall where the hand touched.
6. Body should be streamlined, one hand on top of the other, for the push-off.

Evaluating Your Progress

1. How far below the water surface are the hips of an efficient backstroker?
   a. 1-3 inches
   b. 3-6 inches
   c. 6-8 inches
2. Where is the backstroker's hand when it enters the water?
   a. Directly over the head
   b. Directly over the shoulder
   c. To the side 12 inches from the midline of the body
3. How is the underwater action of the backstroke arms best described?
   a. Pull straight through
   b. Bend the elbow of the pulling arm and press straight through
   c. Bend the elbow of the pulling arm and pull with an "S" stroke
4. What part of the backstroker's lower body breaks the water?
   a. The entire foot
   b. The knee
   c. The big toe

5. Number the following actions to indicate the proper sequence following the backstroke start.
   ________Arm pull
   ________Start of kicking motion
   ________Head positioning
6. How would you describe the touch preceding the backstroke turn?
   a. Touch the wall at the water surface.
   b. Touch the wall 8-12 inches below the surface.
   c. Touch the wall at the easiest place for you.
7. List the points to emphasize when swimmers are streamlining after pushing off on the start or the turn.

Chapter 4: The Breaststroke

Coaching Objectives for the Breaststroke

At the conclusion of this chapter, you should understand how to effectively teach the breaststroke to beginning swimmers. This chapter presents the following:

- Helpful terms referring to the breaststroke.
- Body position, armstroke, kick, and breathing for the breaststroke.
- Coaching points to be emphasized in the breaststroke.
- Drills for learning and developing the breaststroke.
- Starts and turns appropriate for the breaststroke.
- Coaching points to be emphasized in breaststroke starts and turns.

Helpful Terms

Traditional breaststroke. A breaststroke characterized by a flat body position and shoulders that are underwater at all times.

Natural breaststroke. A breaststroke characterized by an up-and-down motion of the head and shoulders and a breath that is taken late in the stroke.

Recovery. The phase of the stroke when the arms and legs have finished the propulsive movement and are returning to the glide position.

Whip kick. The whip-style leg action that is used by breaststrokers.

Feet set. A foot position for the breaststroke in which the toes are not pointed as in other strokes. Instead, they are turned out and flexed at the ankle joint before the backward thrust.

Body Position

The breaststroke body position is in transition from one in which the swimmer is flat in the water to one in which the swimmer moves up and down with a dolphin-like movement. The body positions used in the traditional and natural breaststroke are presented in Figures 4-1 to 4-3 and the following diagrams.

The traditional breaststroke was swum by Chet Jastremski, American record holder in the 1960s. It is the stroke taught in American Red Cross swimming classes. Because most novice competitors progress from beginner swimming lessons, they will know the traditional breaststroke. Coaches will therefore find it easier to teach the elements of the traditional stroke. The natural breaststroke as swum by David Wilkie and Tracy Caulkins, record holders in the 1970s, is very successful with year-round swimmers. From the differences identified in Figure 4-1, you should be able to identify the natural breaststroke. Occasionally, novices will do this stroke. If a young swimmer is successfully performing it, do not change the technique.

	Traditional	Natural
Fig. 4-1 Body Position	Body remains flat in the water.	Body is angled as the hips move up and down.

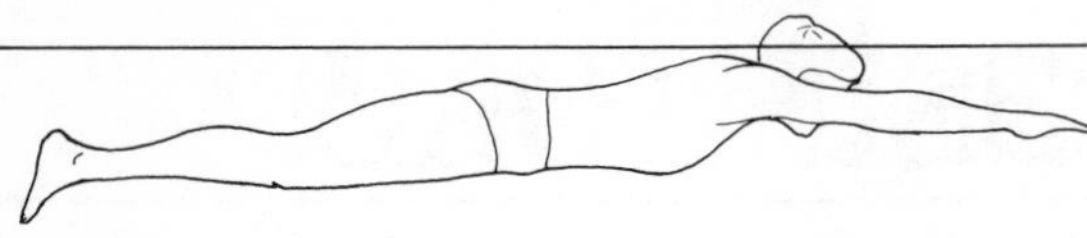

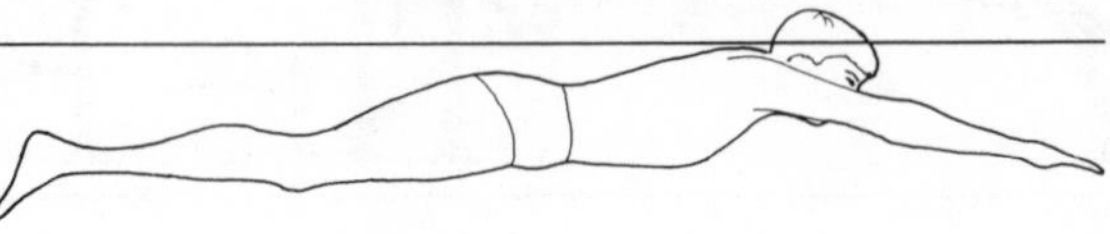

Fig. 4-2 Breathing	The chin is lifted; only the head pivots on the neck.	The head remains stationary, the hips drop, and the head and neck come above the water for a high breath.

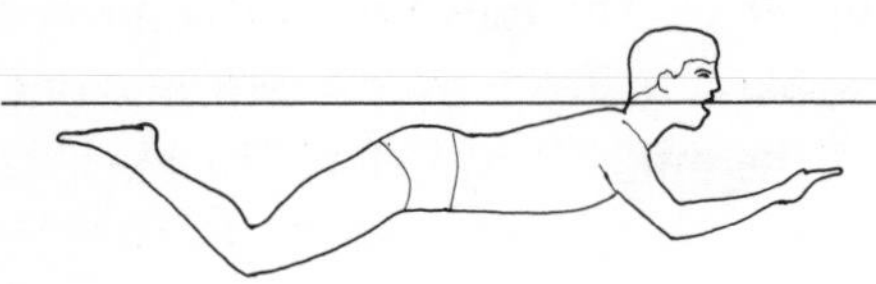

Fig. 4-3 Timing	The breath is taken as the arms come to a point under the shoulders.	The breath is taken as the arms begin to recover to the front

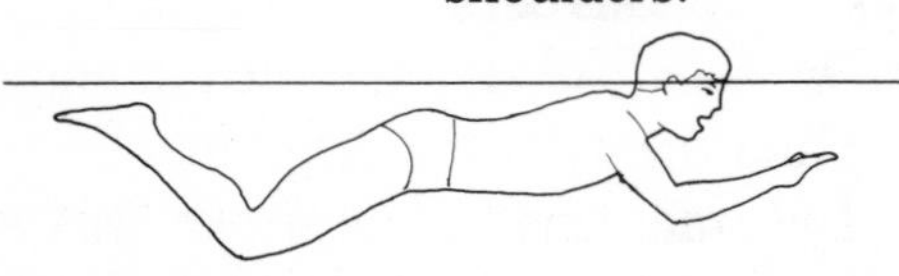

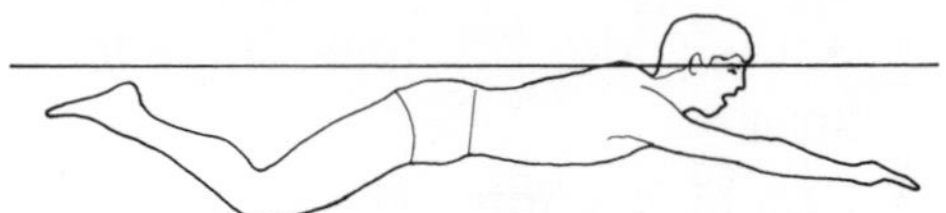

According to swimming rules for the breaststroke, the body must remain on the breast with both shoulders in the horizontal plane. These rules also specify that some portion of the head must be higher than the normal flat surface of the water except on the start and on the strokes before and after the turns.

Fig. 4-4

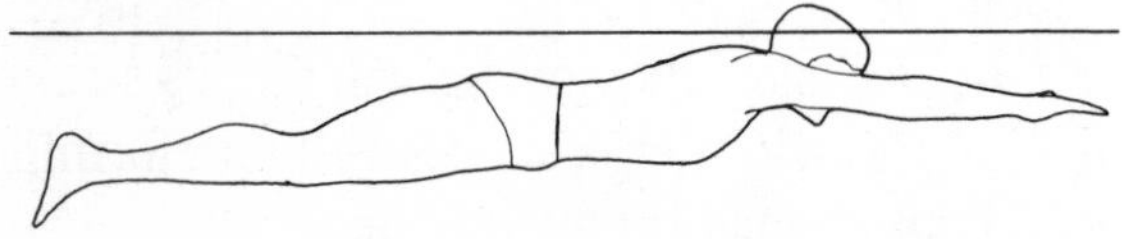

Tell your swimmers to imagine that they are swimming through a pipe. Then the body will stay as flat as possible in the water and resistance will be reduced. Only the top of the head should be above the water surface (see Figure 4-4).

Breaststroke Armstroke

Your swimmers must be aware of the rule that both hands must be pushed forward and brought back simultaneously on or under the surface of the water. When instructing your swimmers in the armstroke, have them begin the pull with the elbows straight and the palms of the hands facing diagonally outward (see Figure 4-5).

Fig. 4-5

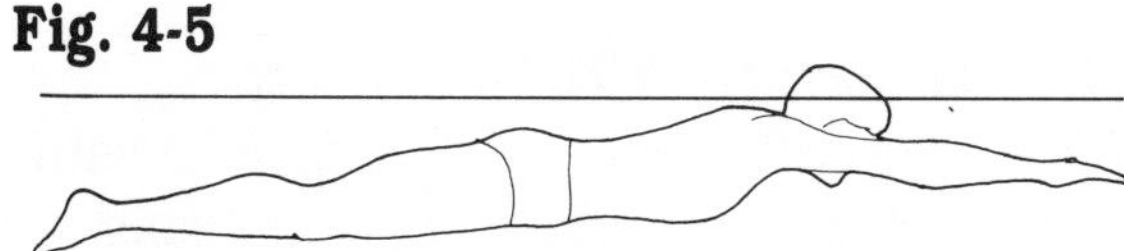

Next, the elbows bend so that they are up as the hands are pulled outward, backward, and downward to just below the shoulders (see Figure 4-6).

Fig. 4-6

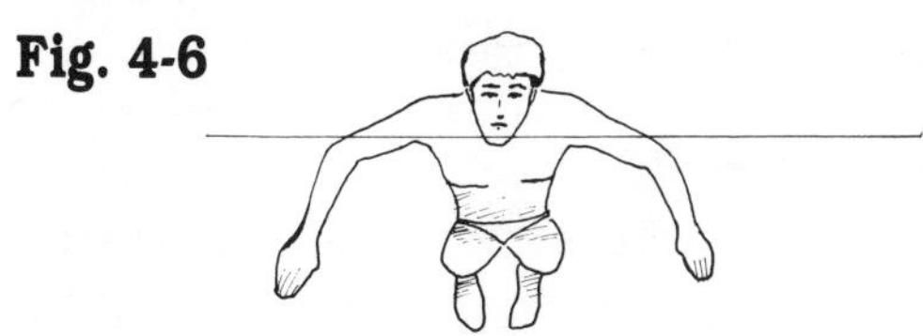

Tell your swimmers to move the hands diagonally inward as the head is lifted for a breath (see Figure 4-7). Then the hands meet and start forward to a fully extended position.

Fig. 4-7

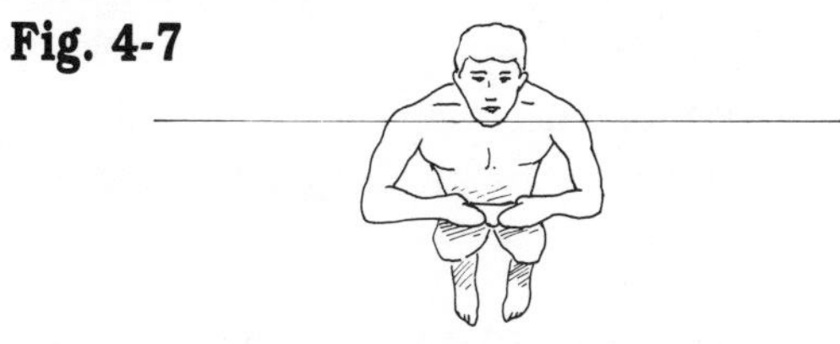

As they swim the breaststroke, swimmers should feel they are drawing a heart or eyeglass shape with their hands (see Figure 4-8).

Fig. 4-8

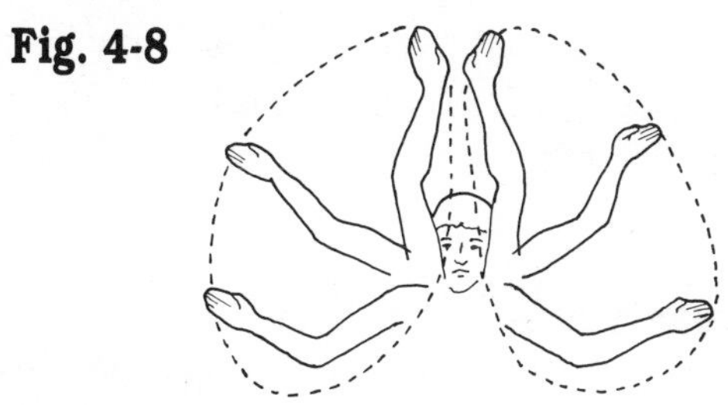

Coaching Points for the Armstroke

1. Start the pull from a streamlined position.
2. Elbows should be up as you pull.
3. The path of the hands should form a heart shape.

The Breaststroke Kick

Swimming rules for the breaststroke specify that the feet must be drawn up with the knees bent and that the movement of the legs and feet must be simultaneous and in the same horizontal plane. No butterfly kick or scissors action that uses the top of the foot or front of the leg is permitted.

First have your swimmers practice the kick supporting themselves against a wall. From an extended position, tell them to bring the heels up towards the buttocks by flexing the hips and knees (see Figure 4.9).

Fig. 4-9

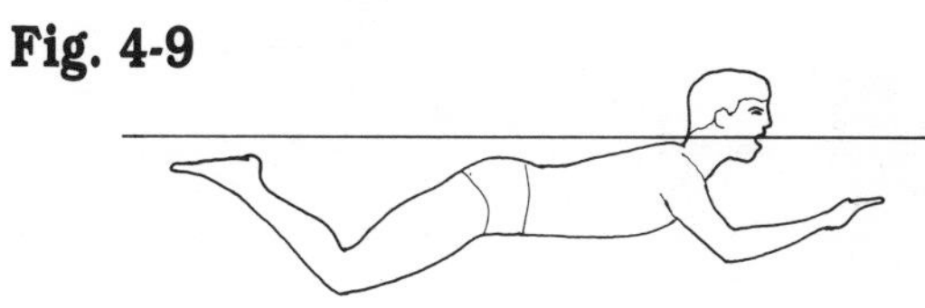

Next, the ankles are flexed with the feet set outward. The feet now return to extension by pushing downward and backward as shown in Figure 4.10

Fig. 4-10

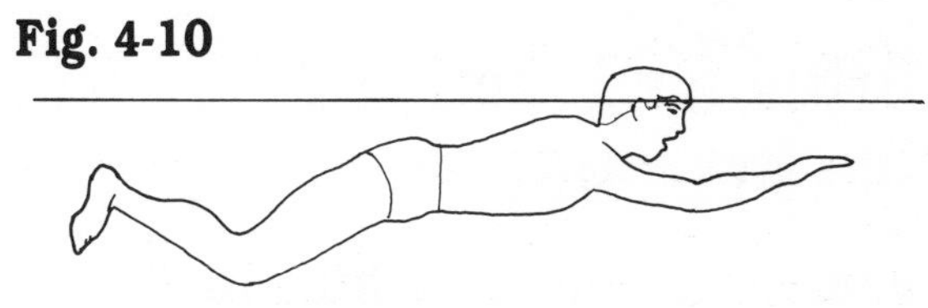

After your swimmer can perform the kick easily, coordinate the kick to the pull by telling your swimmers that the arms start first and the kick starts when the hands start the rounded portion of the heart-shaped path. The arms start to pull again just as the legs finish the kick. This kick provides the main propulsive force in the traditional breaststroke.

Coaching Points for the Breaststroke Kick

1. The feet should be set out as the heels are brought up.
2. Bend legs at the hips as well as the knees.
3. Push feet downward as well as backward.

Breaststroke Breathing Pattern

In the breaststroke breathing pattern, the head is lifted for the breath as the hands come to a point under the breast and the shoulders are at their highest point in the water. The chin remains in the water while the neck is hyperextended to lift only the mouth above the water level (see Figure 4-11).

Fig. 4-11

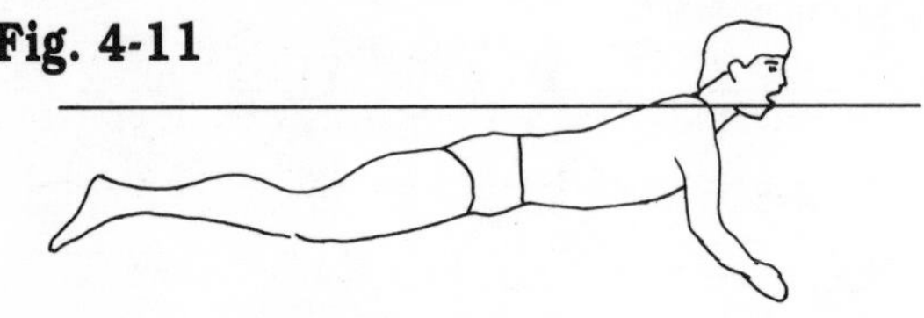

Tell your swimmers to return the face to the water and begin exhaling as the arms begin to return to extension. The chin is tucked, but the top of the head breaks the water line.

Drills for Practicing the Breaststroke

Armstroke and Breathing Drills

(4.1) Armstroke Land Drill

Swimmers stand on the deck and are given a count for each part of the arm pull. On the count of *one*, the swimmers extend both arms fully at shoulder height in front of the chin with the thumbs touching. On *two*, the hands separate and pull outward, downward, and backward to the shoulders. The elbows should be bent and up, with the hands apart slightly more than shoulder width. On *three*, the thumbs come together, and on *four* the arms extend to the position they were in at the count of *one*.

(4.2) Armstroke With Kick Board

Have your swimmers try the armstroke with a kickboard between their legs. Crossing the ankles will keep the board in place. When they can do this correctly, add the breathing pattern to the drill by having the swimmers lift the head after the hands finish the outward phase of the stroke. Stress to your swimmers that their elbows should be up and that their hands should follow a heart-shaped path.

Kicking Drills

(4.3) Breaststroke Kicking With a Board

Have your swimmers practice the kick with the board held in the same positions as shown for the freestyle kick in Figures 2.7 to 2.10.

(4.4) Breaststroke Kicking on the Back

Your swimmers will enjoy doing this drill as a warm-up, or it may be used as a teaching drill. After your swimmers understand the kick, tell them to try it on the back with their hands by their sides, bringing the heels to the buttocks on each kick.

(4.5) Breaststroke Kicking Without a Board

Have your swimmers lie in a prone position with their hands at their sides. The feet are then pulled up or set in the dorsi-flexed position. Tell your swimmers to touch the feet with the hands before they are thrust back. The head may be in the water or above it. If the head is in the water, the breath is taken after the hands touch the feet and before the thrust of the kick.

(4.6) Breaststroke for Power

Use this drill when working on stroke mechanics and body position. First emphasize to your swimmers that they should get as much power as possible from the kick. Next, ask them to count their strokes while trying to swim the pool using as few strokes as possible (10-12 strokes in a 25-yard pool is better than average for swimmers

10 years of age; 7-9 strokes for older recreational swimmers).

Breaststroke Start

Swimming rules allow one arm pull and one leg kick underwater following the start and the turn. However, a portion of the contestant's head must break the surface of the water before another stroke is started. The same grab start used in the freestyle is also used in the breaststroke. For the breaststroke start, instruct your swimmers to drop the head earlier and to dive deeper than for the freestyle but with the same streamlined position.

Tell your swimmers to hold the position following the dive for at least three counts (see figure 4.12). Then, when they feel their momentum decrease, the arms should begin to pull, with the elbows bending to 60 degrees to bring the hands toward the hips, as shown in Figure 4.13.

Fig. 4-12

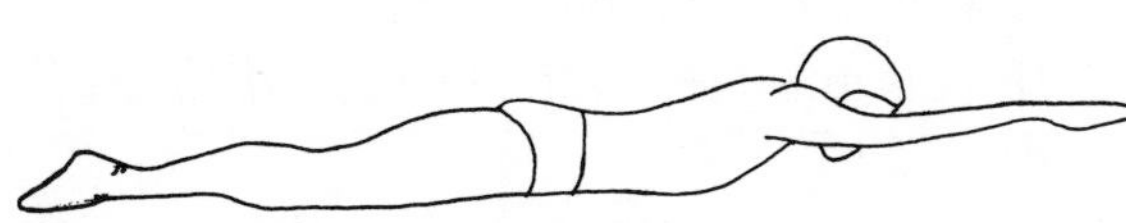

Fig. 4-13

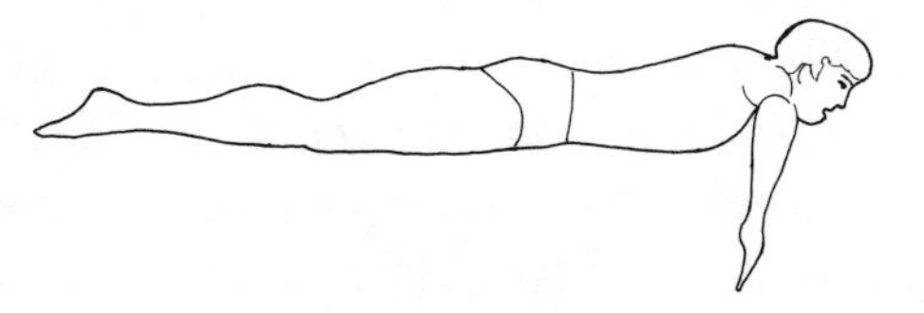

Now the hands accelerate in a fast, whip-like action as the arms are extended. Your swimmers will know the pull is complete when the palms of the hands are directly alongside the body (see Figure 4-14). They should then hold this position for about two counts.

Fig. 4-14

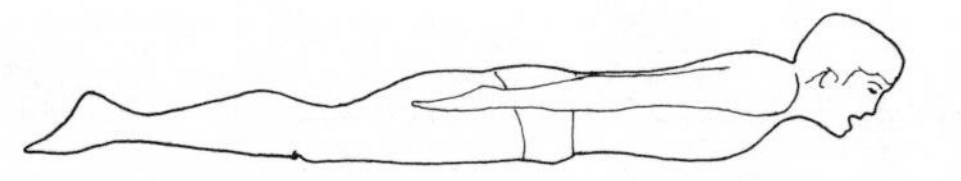

Swimmers recover the arms and legs at the same time. The hands and elbows are kept close to the body to minimize drag, and the head is lifted as the knees are flexed to begin the kick. The arms are extended overhead with the hands below the surface as the legs thrust backwards. Tell your swimmers to check that the head is at the surface to be legally ready for the next stroke (see Figure 4-15).

Fig. 4-15

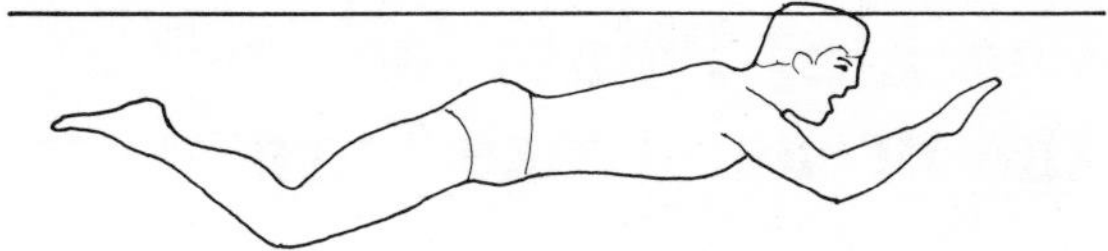

Coaching Points for the Breaststroke Start

1. Hold the streamlined position after the dive.
2. Pull all the way through with the elbows high.
3. Be sure that the head is at the surface before separating the hands for the next stroke.

Breaststroke Turn

Swimming rules state that when touching the end of the pool at the turns or in finishing a race, swimmers must touch with *both hands simultaneously* either at or above the water level. As the swimmer touches the wall or grabs the gutter with both hands, the knees are drawn up to the abdomen. The feet move toward the hips in a straight line just under the body, and the swimmer pivots the hips towards the wall. The hands come off the gutter as the feet are placed on the wall 18 to 24 inches below the surface. Swimmers should be told to leave the wall on their side but to return to the abdomen while extending in the streamlined position with both arms overhead (see Figure 4-16), as discussed in the guidelines for freestyle and backstroke turns. Explain that in contrast to the crawl, in the breaststroke push-off the head is held down, and the swimmer is 2 to 3 feet below the water surface. As on

Fig. 4-16

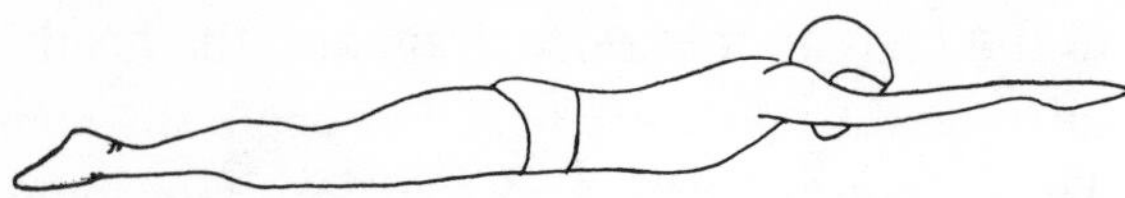

the start, the streamlined position is held until the body begins to lose forward momentum, whereupon the swimmer uses the underwater stroke learned for the start.

Coaching Points for the Breaststroke Turn

1. Touch the wall with both hands simultaneously.
2. Tuck the knees in tight to gain momentum.
3. Push off on the side with the head down.

Evaluating Your Progress

1. The traditional breaststroker is in an extended glide position. Which body part is the first to move for the next stroke?
   a. Head
   b. Legs
   c. Arms
2. What is the correct foot position before the breaststroker thrusts the feet backward?
   a. Ankles are flexed; feet are set in.
   b. Ankles are flexed; feet are set out.
   c. Toes are pointed; feet are set out.
3. When does the traditional breaststroker breathe?
   a. As the hands start the pull.
   b. As the hands move under the shoulders.
   c. During the glide.
4. Which diagram illustrates the correct elbow position?

Fig. 4-17

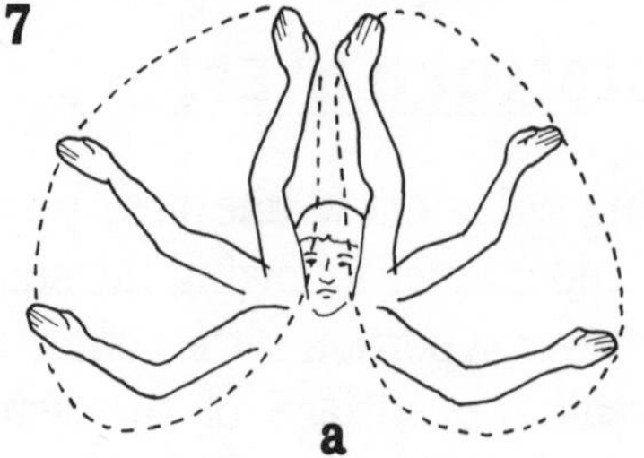

a

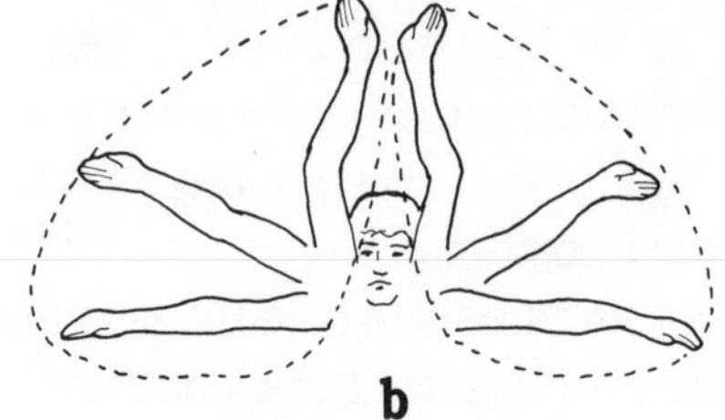

b

5. How long may the breaststroker legally remain underwater after a start or turn?
   a. Only 3 seconds
   b. Only one arm pull
   c. Only one arm pull and one leg kick
6. How is the breaststroker judged to be underwater?
   a. The contestant is underwater until any part of the body breaks the surface of the water.
   b. The contestant is underwater until the head breaks the surface of the water.
7. Is the breaststroker disqualified if an underwater stroke is taken after the start or turn?

Chapter 5: The Butterfly Stroke

Coaching Objectives for the Butterfly

At the conclusion of this chapter, you should understand how to effectively teach the butterfly stroke to beginning swimmers. This chapter presents the following:

- Helpful terms referring to the butterfly.
- Body position, armstroke, kick, and breathing for the butterfly.
- Coaching points to be emphasized in the butterfly.
- Drills for learning and developing the butterfly.
- Starts and turns appropriate for the butterfly.

Helpful Terms

Dolphin kick. An up-and-down undulating movement that starts at the hips and ends with a fishtail motion at the feet.
Hips up. This signal reminds swimmers to return the hips to a slight pike between each dolphin kick.
Wide elbows. This signal reminds swimmers to keep the elbows pointed out to the side of the pool when the hands are under the chest.
Keyhole pull. The path of the hands during propulsion forming a keyhole shape.
Push phase. The end of the propulsive phase when the hands accelerate.
Individual medley. Often termed the IM. This event includes all four strokes. The butterfly is the first stroke of this event, followed by the backstroke, the breaststroke, and finally the freestyle.

Body Position

Have your swimmers start the butterfly stroke in a prone position. Tell your swimmers to keep their legs together, with the arms extended overhead and the eyes focused on the bottom of the pool. Explain that the head position will change with the kick.

The Butterfly Armstroke

The butterfly arm pull can best be learned in shallow water with the body bent at the hips and the feet on the bottom of the pool. Swimmers begin with the arms straight overhead and the hands several inches below the surface of the water. The arms are then pressed downward and outward with the elbows high and bent (see Figure 5-1).

Fig. 5-1

Describe the path of the arm pull to your swimmers as drawing a keyhole. After the outward pull, the hands continue around and toward the chest, thus forming the top of the keyhole. The hands are now close together with the thumbs almost touching under the chest. The hands then press to the hips, forming the bottom of the keyhole (see Figure 5-2).

Fig. 5-2

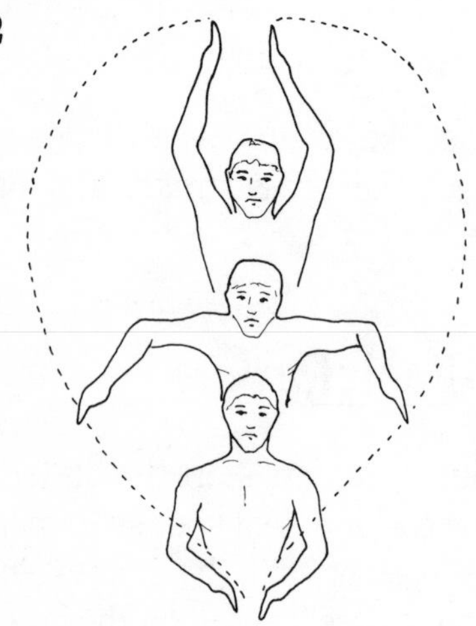

If your swimmers accelerate their hands during the push phase of the stroke, they will eliminate the feeling that some swimmers have of getting their hands stuck under their hips. On the recovery, the arms are swung over the surface of the water with the elbows almost straight. The hands enter the water shoulder-width apart (see Figure 5-3).

Fig. 5-3

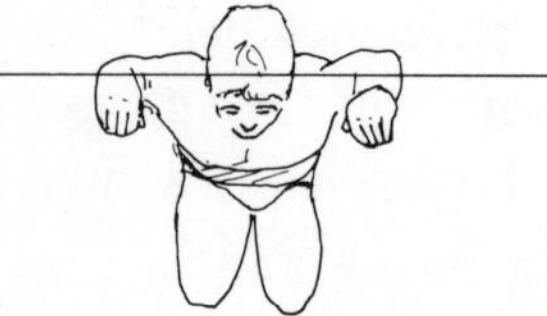

The Butterfly Kick

After your swimmers can do the armstroke in shallow water, teach them the butterfly kick. If your swimmers have access to fins, now is the time to use them. Teach kicking in the prone position with the fins on and the hands behind the back. Your swimmers may pretend they are Houdini with their hands tied behind their backs and their ankles tied together with imaginary rope. They must propel themselves across the pool while keeping both legs together and moving in the vertical plane. This kick actually originates with an undulating motion of the swimmer's torso. The hips are high as the straight legs are brought upward in the water as shown in Figure 5-4.

Fig. 5-4

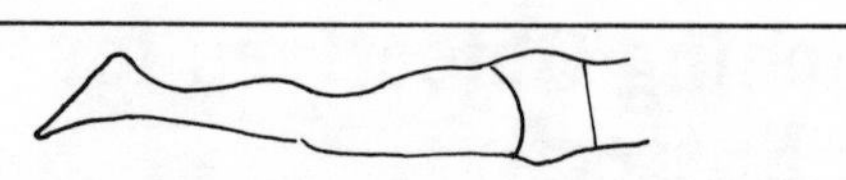

As the swimmer's heels reach the surface of the water, the hips sink and the knees bend (see Figure 5-5).

Fig. 5-5

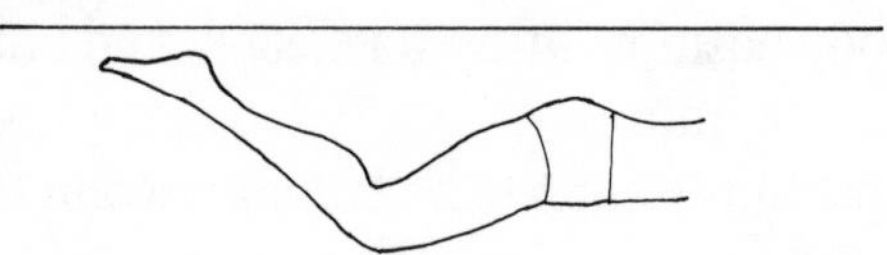

Now the hips are brought up again, causing the legs to straighten in much the same way that the end of a rope is snapped straight (see Figure 5-6).

Fig. 5-6

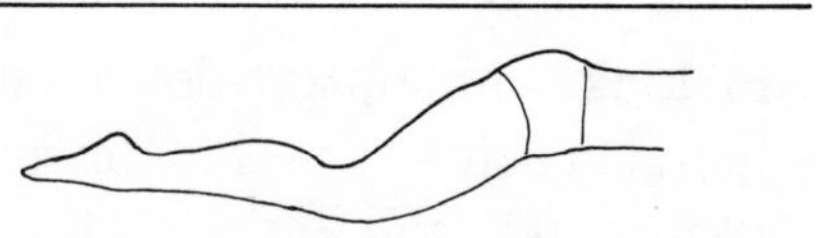

Again the hips are high and the heels are low, ready to repeat the motion as shown in Figure 5-7.

Fig. 5-7

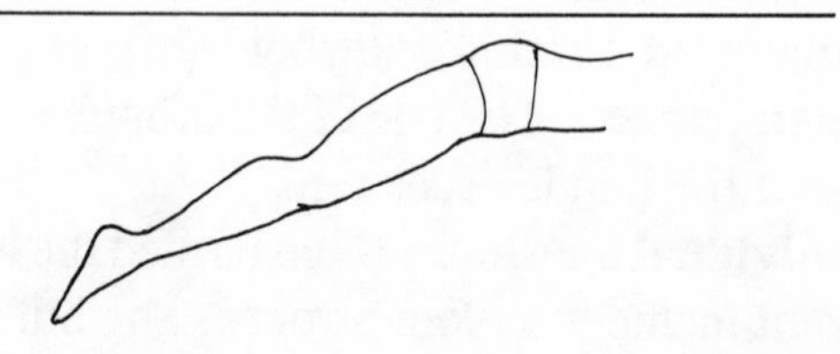

For your younger swimmers introduce the butterfly kick as a game of pretend. The swimmer is a bucking bronco trying to get a cowboy off his back. This imagery will encourage the upward and downward snapping action of the body. Learning swimmers should lift their feet or the tips of their fins out of the water on every kick. This is an exaggeration, but it promotes the right body movements.

The armstroke and kick may be done together for a short distance in shallow water before your swimmers learn to breathe. Two kicks are taken for each stroke. The first downbeat occurs when the hands are at the lower part of the keyhole, accelerating to recover. The second kick drives the arms into the round part of the keyhole.

Butterfly Breathing Pattern

Have your swimmers elevate the head by pulling the chin forward when they breathe. If the breath is timed properly, the chin will remain in the water during the inhalation phase of the stroke. The butterfly breathing pattern is best described as a forward lean rather than as a lift of the head (see Figure 5-8).

Fig. 5-8

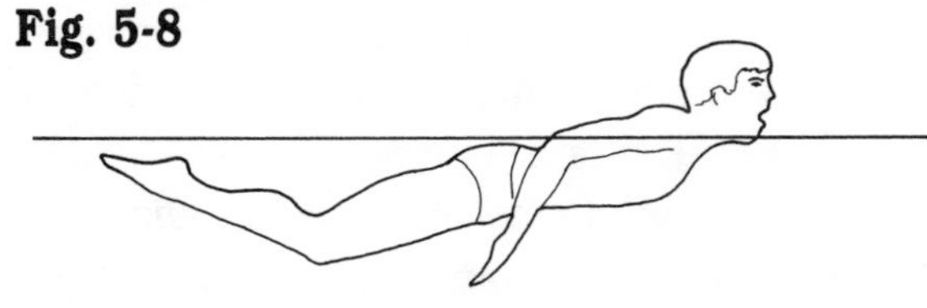

Because most young swimmers have trouble knowing where their arms are, many coaches time the breath to the kick. The inhalation is taken at the bottom of the keyhole as the feet take their first kick. The exhalation occurs with the chin tucked and the face toward the bottom of the pool at the same time as the second kick. Most good swimmers breathe only every other stroke.

Drills for Practicing the Butterfly Stroke

Drills are of the greatest importance when novice swimmers are learning and practicing the butterfly. The physical characteristics of 8-, 9-, and 10-year-olds necessitate a different approach to the butterfly with young swimmers than is used at the college level. Young swimmers have thin necks, heads that are disproportionately large for their bodies, and higher centers of gravity than adults. Breathing is therefore difficult for youngsters if the stroke is swum for a long distance. Drills are more effective, encourage better stroke techniques, and are better for morale than the complete butterfly stroke.

Armstroke and Breathing Drills

(5.1) Mirror Drill

The mirror drill teaches timing and the proper armstroke. Have your swimmers stand in front of a mirror and bend forward. Now have them practice the butterfly armstroke noticing that the hands are pulled back in the keyhole motion as the head is lifted for the breath. The head is then lowered as the hands complete the recovery. Have your swimmers check the timing of the head and the motion of the arms in the mirror while saying the word *kick* at the appropriate time.

(5.2) Butterfly With a Kickboard

Have your swimmers hold the board in front of them with only the hands on the board. The arms should be straight, and the face should be in the water. Tell them to keep one hand on the board while the other hand performs the armstroke motion. Breathing and kicking are performed with the proper timing. Alternate the stroking arms.

(5.3) One-Arm Butterfly

This drill teaches the butterfly armstroke and timing. Swimmers perform the exercise with one hand overhead at all times. The other hand pulls through with the proper motion. The breath is taken to the side. However, the swimmer drives the head below the water surface before the recovering arm enters the water. Be sure that your swimmers keep the arm recovery high, with the elbow almost straight to give momentum and encourage the head to dive. The hips may pivot to the side, causing the kick to be on the side, but the correct rhythm of two kicks per stroke is maintained. This drill may be varied by doing three strokes with the right arm followed by three strokes with the left or by doing one stroke with the right arm, one with the left, and then one with both arms. This drill should *not* be done with the arm sequence left, right, left, right because this causes the swimmer to use the bent arm recovery of the crawl stroke.

Dolphin Kicking Drills

(5.4) Underwater Undulation
To help your swimmers gain total body movement, have them completely submerge in waist-deep water. Holding their breath, tell your swimmers to push off the wall with the arms at the sides. Using the head to initiate the dolphin-like body motion, the swimmers kick their legs up and down to utilize the full flexion of the body. After four to six kicks, bending from the knees and kicking equally up and down with the whole body, they surface for a quick breath of air by lifting the head to the surface and then back down into the water.

(5.5) Kicking on the Side
To strengthen the kick and prepare your swimmers for the one-arm butterfly, have them lie on their sides with the hand closer to the bottom of the pool extended over the head. Tell your swimmers to place the other hand by the side and dolphin kick as shown in Figure 5-9.

Fig. 5-9

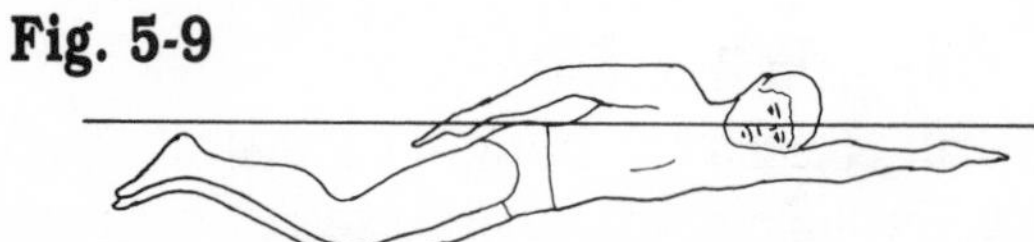

(5.6) Kicking With a Board
The board must be held with both hands on top of the lower third of the board. The swimmer's face is in the water. The hips and soles of the feet come to the surface of the water. The feet are then flicked downward so that the backs of the knees lead to the surface. This drill teaches the dolphin-like kicking action, and because the swimmers' heads are close to the surface, they can breathe easily or be stopped for corrections if necessary.

Butterfly Starts

The butterfly start is done exactly as the freestyle start. As in the freestyle, swimmers streamline after the start. In the butterfly start, however, swimming rules require both arms to be recovered over the surface of the water. As in the freestyle, teach your swimmers not to breathe until they have taken a few strokes.

Butterfly Turns

The butterfly turn is performed like the breaststroke turn with two hands touching the wall at the same time. For the butterfly turn, however, the feet are not planted on the wall as deep as they are for the breaststroke.

Tell your swimmers that the feet should be crossed as they are brought toward the wall and are placed about 1 foot below water level. The body pivots on the hips, and the upper arm swings forward over the water as the lower arm is pushed forward underwater. The hands reach to streamline as the push-off begins with the body on the side but rotating to the stomach so that the shoulders are level by the time the feet leave the wall on the push-off. Because the armstroke recovery in the butterfly must be over the surface of the water, the underwater stroke is not used but the first stroke off the wall should be taken with the face in the water.

Evaluating Your Progress

1. How many downbeats of the legs are taken for each butterfly armstroke?
   a. One
   b. Two
   c. Three
2. Which phrase best describes the inhalation phase of the butterfly?
   a. Chin forward and in the water
   b. Chin lifted and out of the water
3. Which phrase would you use to correct a straight arm butterflyer?
   a. "Push hands"
   b. "Wide elbows"
   c. "S pull"
4. Which signal will help your swimmers if they have trouble recovering their arms?
   a. "Lift as you recover."
   b. "Recover to the side."
   c. "Accelerate your hands during the push phase of the stroke."
5. Your young swimmers dislike the butterfly. How would you improve their performance in this stroke?
   a. Do not do the butterfly until they are stronger.
   b. Insist they do the butterfly a little each day.
   c. Use drills and the modified butterfly in practice.

Swimming Planning Guide

Now that you know how to teach swimming strokes and techniques you are probably eager to begin practice sessions. But unless you know how to design and conduct practices, your enthusiasm could end in frustration. To conduct an effective practice requires careful planning. Take the time to study this Planning Guide section of *Coaching Swimming Effectively* and you will find practices more beneficial and enjoyable for your players—and for you.

Included in this section are sample practice plans for the beginning, middle, and end of the season. These sample plans have been designed as guides to help you conduct practices. Although they can be used as written, they can and should be altered to best meet the needs of your swimmers.

Chapter 6: Preseason Planning

Coaching Objectives for the Preseason

At the conclusion of this chapter, you should be able to utilize correct information and appropriate procedures for preparing for a competitive season. The necessary preseason coaching tasks include the following:

- Acquiring information pertinent to your coaching situation.
- Developing seasonal goals appropriate for your team.
- Formulating specific goals for each part of your team's season.
- Establishing a policy for awards.
- Determining the authority that should be delegated.
- Selecting the necessary equipment.

Surveying the Situation

Organizing your season is the first step to success. In order to plan, you must have the answers to six questions that will determine the most appropriate training program for your athletes.

1. *What is the background of the potential swimmers?*
   To answer this question, talk to people who have previously been associated with the program. What will be the swimmers' ages? With what programs have they been associated? In what other sports or team situations have they participated? A wide diversity in age and experience may prompt you to divide your workout time so that swimmers practice with others of similar backgrounds and ability levels.
2. *How much pool time is available?*
   The amount of available pool time will to some extent determine your team's goals. Expecting to win a state high school championship is unrealistic if your swimmers are only in the pool for 45 minutes a day, 5 days a week. However, you may be able to have a successful season by joining a league with other schools in the same situation. These decisions must be made before the season begins.
3. *How many swimmers will be training per lane?*
   Determine the approximate number of swimmers through a sign up procedure or by checking previous attendance records. Divide the number of swimmers by the number of lanes in your pool to determine the number of swimmers per lane. The number of swimmers per lane will influence the types of things you can do, the maximum lengths of continuous swimming, and whether you will need more than one practice session each day to accommodate all swimmers.
4. *What governing body determines the rules and regulations?*
   Does your team belong to a league? If so, are preseason meetings held for the coaches? Is there a written set of rules? What are your team's responsibilities as a league member,

and what are the benefits of league membership?

5. *What are the dates of the biggest meets?* Early information about the season's major meets tells you what you are working toward and the pace you will need to maintain. When you know the date of the biggest meet or championship, you can designate the 2 weeks before this date for meet preparation. This period of preparation is called the *taper*. Of the remaining time prior to the championship meet, allocate 30% for early season training, 35% for midseason work, and 35% for late season work. Mark the starting date of each part of the season on your calendar before the season begins. Keep the championship meet at the end of your dual meet season with no other meets after this culminating event.
6. *In what events will your swimmers be participating?* You must know the events for which your swimmers are training. In some summer leagues, the dominant events are 25- and 50-yard events. In high school, 100-yard and 200-yard events are common. Your training program will be dictated by the distances to be swum in competition. For example, if most competition will be in the shorter events, more work should be done on sprinting.

The preceding six questions should be answered before opening your season and, in fact, even before you accept a coaching position. If adjustments must be made in the above areas, the preseason is the time to determine exactly what needs to be done.

Developing Long-Term Goals

The next step is to address the decisions that will establish the team's direction for the season. Goals will vary with each individual coach and situation, but a realistic set of team goals that encompasses more than winning meets is an important base for any team and coach. By considering possible goals, potential coaches should be able to decide upon goals that match their coaching situations and swimmers' personalities.

The following general goals should be evident to parents and participants:

- To offer healthy activity.
- To develop mental and physical discipline.
- To provide opportunity for social adjustment and exposure.
- To recognize accomplishment.
- To offer a constructive use of leisure time.
- To develop talent.
- To provide fun.

Shortly after starting the very successful David Douglas Swim Team, Don Jacklin (1973) stated his goals in *Swimming World* as the following:

1. To encourage youngsters of all abilities to compete in the program, allowing each individual to develop to his or her full potential.
2. To encourage individual goal-setting.
3. To spend as much time as possible on a one-to-one basis with each youngster on goal-setting, values, future plans in life, and anything else they want to discuss emphasizing the whole person (pp. 23-25).

The above goals are very broad. Nevertheless, they can be developed specifically by teaching children how to race, including race strategy and pace. Through consistent effort to improve their own performance, your swimmers will begin to develop competitiveness and mental toughness—the ability to perform well under stress.

The goal of proper stroke technique must also be considered because this will lead to improved times, increased self-discipline, and greater self-esteem.

Take time during the preseason to develop your personal goals for your team. Well-developed goals and priorities will enable you to give logical answers to parents' and swimmers' questions about your program. Refer to your goals later in the season when you have decisions to make. This policy will develop fairness and consistency within your program.

Developing Short-Term Goals

Your next step in planning is to develop short-term goals for each part of the season. You have designated dates on your calendar to mark the beginning and ending of the early season, mid-season, late season, and taper. Now consider what must be accomplished during each designated time period.

Early Season

The first third of your swimming season should stress learning the proper stroke mechanics, and developing strength, endurance, and flexibility. These are the essential components needed to improve in swimming. Additionally, you should introduce swimmers to the equipment they will use, to the terminology specific to swimming, and help them to set meaningful goals that they can accomplish.

Teaching Proper Stroke Techniques

When you consider the shortness of each recreational swimming season and recreational practice sessions, conditioning cannot be as major a factor in a recreational program as it is in a year-round program. Therefore, the single factor that will most improve a recreational swimmer's time is improved technique. Only when swimmers can "hold their strokes" (i.e., execute a series properly) should they attempt distance work. Meanwhile, you may use kicking series with boards to improve your swimmers' endurance.

Improving Strength, Endurance, and Flexibility

The results of a dryland exercise program will not be obvious for 6 weeks after you begin the program with your swimmers. It will, however, improve your swimmer's speed and give you something to do on cold, rainy early-season mornings or when the pool is unavailable. It will also establish the fact that practice will always be held and eliminate phone calls on questionable days. Because the dryland exercise program is the one time your swimmers are working with their heads out of the water, it is also an excellent time for communication. Therefore, besides building strength, endurance, and flexibility, you can use this opportunity to establish swimmers' personal goals, share their interests, and generally enjoy being with them.

Introducing Swimmers to Training Equipment

How to read a pace clock, how to swim in circles, and how to use training aids such as flutter boards and goggles are essential skills to be learned by all team members.

Presenting a Swimming Vocabulary

For ease of communication and understanding, all of your swimmers should comprehend two new vocabularies. One includes the terms you will use to correct your swimmers' movements and describe certain stroke adjustments; the second includes universally recognized terms such as those in the glossary at the end of this manual. These terms will help your swimmers to understand what is happening at meets and to communicate with other swimming enthusiasts.

Helping Your Swimmers to Set Appropriate, Meaningful Goals

You can best help your swimmers to set appropriate goals by communicating your own goals with statements such as "I saw lots of crawl flip turns in practice today. I hope tomorrow everyone will try them at every opportunity."

Midseason

The next third of your season, the midseason, is the time to increase the workload of your swimmers so they develop the capacity to compete vigorously. Included in this process is perfecting the armstroke, breathing, kicking and turning techniques for each racing stroke. Also, because your swimmers will begin competitions you will need to foster a team spirit and camaraderie among your swimmers.

Increasing Your Swimmers' Endurance

The distances swum in the early season should be gradually increased by 50%. This goal is not easily accomplished because while you increase the distance you must continue to demand proper stroke techniques and, most importantly, keep the practices fun and interesting.

Perfecting Turning Techniques

Demand that your swimmers make proper turns at every wall. At this point parents often complain, "You never practice turns anymore, and my child needs this practice." Group endurance will suffer if you stop to have your entire team drill turns. You've just spent the early season, which is 30% of the total season, teaching proper techniques. The answer to this dilemma is obvious when you consider that a team of swimmers over 10 years of age is probably swimming 3,000 yards a day. That distance represents 120 lengths of a 25-yard pool, a minimum of 100 turns a day. If you insist that each turn be done well and work individually with swimmers who cannot yet do them correctly, your team will make good turns and develop the reputation of being a "well-coached" team.

Improving Racing Techniques

Many of your competitions will be held during the midseason, so end each practice session with some swims of 25 yards or less, starting with a dive and ending with a turn. Vary this with one-length relays or swim widths.

Developing Team Spirit

Team spirit develops when a coach cares about the team members and the team members care about each other and the coach. This feeling will begin during the early season, but conscious effort and preseason planning will be needed if the spirit is to continue through the busy midseason. When you announce your meet schedule, announce a team function to be held during the midseason. The details can be attended to later by team members, but if the date is not announced well in advance, some members of the team will be unable to attend. Also plan ahead for inexpensive items that will give your team identity. Pins or balloons with team slogans are inexpensive but must be ordered in advance. A company or chamber of commerce that gives away items for their own advertising might be willing to provide items appropriate for your team at little or no cost.

Late Season

The next third of your season, the late season, you should help your swimmers develop a sense of pace during races and help them cope with the stress of a long season that ends with championship races.

Helping Swimmers Gain a Sense of Pace

Goal-oriented long swims divided into shorter, linked intervals or broken swims and repetition training involving hard efforts at near top speed with long rest intervals are two ways to develop your swimmers' sense of pace and increase their mental toughness.

Encouraging Swimmers to Handle Stress

The increased emphasis in practice on performing certain times puts your swimmers under stress in an environment where you, the coach, can provide guidance on stress management. Self-acceptance by the swimmers when they cannot perform should be emphasized as strongly as the determination to improve.

Taper Season

The last 2 weeks of your season, the taper, is when the swimmer's body is allowed to make its final adaptation in preparation for the most important competition of the season. Thus, the taper should be pointed to the biggest or championship meet; usually the last swimming event of the season. The following three goals should be emphasized during the taper season. You should emphasize peaking or swimming as fast as possible by resting, focusing on competition, and enjoying alternate activities.

Helping Swimmers to Swim Their Fastest Times

During the taper, swimmers in a year-round team would decrease the number of yards they swim. However, your recreational swimmers swim fewer yards in practice than year-round swimmers. Therefore, for recreational swimmers the reduction in work is not as important as the change in activities during the taper. Stop all dryland exercises. Have your swimmers swim pool widths instead of lengths to polish all strokes and give additional practice on starts, turns, and relay starts.

Establishing the Proper Psychological Attitude

Team meetings, gimmicks, and slogans all help to focus the swimmers' attention on their big meets. In preparation, for major competitions urge your swimmers to avoid strenuous activities. Emphasize that your swimmers should get enough rest and stay out of the hot sun for 1 or 2 days before the big meet.

Allowing Time for Enjoyment

Never sacrifice the fun of the taper season to the stress that accompanies competition. If the team goals are set preseason, the extent of the team's accomplishment of these goals will be obvious. The swimmers will know that they are well prepared, and the confidence will be contagious. Thus the final competition will be a positive experience for everyone involved.

Awards

Developing definite criteria before the season opens is your first step to establishing significant awards. Swimmers, like other young people, insist upon fairness and will appreciate awards that are presented on the basis of consistent standards. The athletic director or board of directors for your team should receive your standards and review them preseason. After agreement on the criteria for recognition, swimmers and parents should review and sign a written copy of the standards. Two types of awards are common in recreational swimming: participation awards and achievement awards.

Participation Awards

A participation award is for successful participation in a sport. This award may take the form of inexpensive wearing apparel or emblems that can be acquired only by fulfilling the requirements of team membership. This award shows that the swimmer was a member of a team and met certain obligations to achieve membership on that team. The following are the usual criteria for a team participation award:

- *An attendance requirement*
  The team members may be required to practice a certain number of sessions per week, except when they are excused. These excused absences should be granted only for good cause and only when they are requested personally by the swimmer from the coach *in advance* of the session to be missed. The coach should also grant excused absences on an individual basis if the swimmer appears to be overly tired or ill.
- *A point requirement*
  To receive an award, criteria may require each swimmer to accumulate a specific number of points in dual meets. The number of points required is usually determined by the number of meets in which the team participates and the system used for scoring. One fifth-place showing for each meet could be the minimum requirement for a team with a six-lane pool.
- *Conduct Standards*
  Stipulated conduct and good sportsmanship must be adhered to while the swimmers are representing their school or club. The code would prohibit the use of drugs, alcohol, and tobacco and put forth those standards that are consistent with those within the swimmer's community.

If attendance requirements, point requirements, and conduct standards are presented in writing prior to the beginning of the season, everyone will know what to expect, and postseason complaints will be kept to a minimum.

Achievement Awards

The second type of award is one that signifies outstanding achievement in the sport. Sometimes these awards are made by outside organizations. Any organization wishing to honor a team should make all arrangements through the team's athletic director or governing body. As coach, you should monitor awards to ensure that equal awards are given to boys and girls, that recipients are chosen in an equitable manner (preferably by the coach), and that the value of the award is consistent with the achievement. For example, a 6-inch trophy should not be given to the team's outstanding swimmer while a 10-inch trophy is given to the best 10-year-old because it was donated by a parent.

Presenting outstanding swimmer trophies should be kept to a minimum. A simple certificate given to the most valuable swimmer from each meet is an alternative approach that keeps awards low-key. Certificates can be awarded at a team get-together at the end of the season. As each award is presented, the highlights of the meet can be recalled. Often these certificates will go to your best swimmer, but in some cases you can give the award to a third-place finisher whose improved times inspired other team members or enabled the team to win a crucial point. Plan ahead for these awards and keep notes on meets as you proceed through the season.

If tradition or the organization that you are associated with insists that an outstanding swimmer's trophy be awarded, establish a formal point system. Give points for each practice session attended, for holding a leadership position on the team, for scoring points in dual meets, for having the team's best time in an event, and for holding records. The swimmer accumulating the most points during the season could then be named your outstanding swimmer based on skill, attitude, and leadership.

Delegation of Authority

The coach's ability to delegate authority can be crucial to a team's successful season. In some situations, team managers, secretaries, nonrelated volunteers, or assistant coaches are available. In other situations, only parents are available for the many tasks that are so vital to conducting a competitive program. Your first rule should be to work directly with the swimmers personally and delegate to others those tasks that are not swimmer-related. The following tasks can be delegated to trained and supervised parents or others:

- Running meets.
- Keeping team records and recording swimmers' best times.
- Organizing team get-togethers and awards banquets.
- Organizing transportation.
- Fund raising.
- With some guidance, public relations. (Check all announcements for validity and objectivity.)

The role of assistant coach should *not* be delegated or assumed by team managers, parents, or other untrained volunteers. In fact, parents should be discouraged from walking onto the deck during workouts. This portion of the coach's time belongs to the swimmers. A polite preseason letter on this matter and the phrase, "May I call you about that matter?" to those who ignore your request will solve these problems except with the most persistent parents. Some overly enthusiastic parents will react well if you redirect their energies into other useful projects, but as a final resort you must simply refuse to communicate with parents during workouts.

Equipment

Most swimming programs operate on a limited budget. Therefore, you must carefully decide upon the equipment that is most necessary for your team. Most experienced coaches choose the following items:

- *A pace clock*
  A pace clock gives a coach freedom to walk around, correct strokes, and get involved in the workout instead of standing around reading off times and saying "Ready? Go!" It also encourages swimmers to be aware of their practice times.
- *Kickboards*
  Kickboards allow swimmers to build endurance and improve cardiovascular efficiency even before they can do a stroke for a great distance. Kickboards also allow them to break the stroke into parts so that they can concentrate on and drill the stroke in parts.
- *Backstroke flags*
  Backstroke flags are safety items that allow backstrokers to count their strokes to the wall. As soon as swimmers learn to use the flags, they will improve their backstroke times by not looking over their shoulders as they approach the wall.
- *Lane lines*
  Swimmers must learn to swim in "circles" during practice. Providing lane lines between each group of swimmers is the only way to achieve this formation safely with large numbers of swimmers in a pool.
- *Materials for running meets*
  A starter's gun and ammunition, stop watch, clip board, and pencil for each lane in your pool and proper scoring sheets and cards for recording times are necessary to conduct meets.
- *Record and bulletin boards*
  Record and bulletin boards are important for communication with your team. A record board will help establish goals and provide recognition of accomplishments. A bulletin board will provide information for swimmers and parents.
- *Goggles*
  Goggles have revolutionized swimming by eliminating the eye irritation that frequently bothers competitive swimmers. Although goggles sometimes leak, are difficult to get used to, and are easily lost or broken, they are well worth the cost and trouble of using them. In addition, goggles have become an important safety feature because they encourage swimmers to keep their eyes open and thereby avoid collisions. Each swimmer should personally own one or more sets of goggles.

If resources permit, additional equipment such as paddles, pullbuoys, and flippers are desirable at the recreational level. The following literature is also useful for recreational teams. *Swimmers Magazine* is a bimonthly publication that focuses on techniques employed by successful recreational and year-round swimmers and swim clubs. It has a section for parents of swimmers and articles written by famous swimmers, coaches, and sports psychologists. The magazine may be obtained from *Swimmer's Magazine*, P.O. Box 15906, Nashville, TN 37215.

Swimming World and Junior Swimmer is published monthly and usually offers articles of interest to all water sports enthusiasts. It publishes instructional articles and meet results and explains the training program of national level swimmers. Because the magazine attempts to appeal to a varied audience, some of its articles are of little interest to seasonal swimmers, but most of the articles would be of interest to coaches of seasonal competitive swimmers. It may be obtained from *Swimming World and Junior Swimmer*, P.O. Box 45497, Los Angeles, CA 90045.

In addition to these periodicals, the books listed in the bibliography at the end of this manual are appropriate for further study by seasonal competitive swimming coaches.

Other equipment that may be acquired by swimmers to enhance the team spirit of the sport includes team caps (an inexpensive way to provide team identification), team swim suits, tee shirts, warm-up suits, banners, sport bags, or jackets. All of these items are helpful in establishing team pride and identification but should be recommended before the season to the parents board and be acquired only after their agreement.

Evaluating Your Progress

1. You have been offered the position of head swimming coach at a local country club. List some of the questions you will ask regarding the position.
2. Is each of the following short-term goals most appropriate for the early season, midseason, late season, or taper?
   a. Perfecting turning techniques.
   b. Setting swimmers' personal goals.
   c. Improving strength and flexibility.
   d. Increasing endurance.
   e. Teaching proper stroke and turn techniques.
   f. Peaking physically and psychologically.
   g. Teaching pacing of races.
3. List the long-term goals that are appropriate for a situation in which you would like to coach. Consider your goals again. Are they listed from highest to lowest priority?
4. List your requirements for a participation award.
5. Discuss an acceptable policy for excusing swimmers from practice.
6. How does a coach determine the recipient of an award for the team's outstanding swimmer?
7. In order of importance, list the equipment you would require to coach a recreational swim team.

Chapter 7: Early Season Planning

At the conclusion of this chapter, you should be able to employ correct information for the following early season coaching tasks:

- Helping swimmers set their individual goals for the season.
- Presenting a dryland exercise program for your swimmers following accepted basic principles.
- Teaching techniques useful to swimmers in their first workout.
- Preparing workouts that employ proper training techniques for the early season.

Setting Individual Goals

Personal swimming goals are the product of a swimmer's background, commitment to the sport, and emotional maturity and of the coach's input. Goals tell the swimmers where they are going and what they have accomplished when they get there. Goals must be established on an individual basis early in the season. This may be done by passing out note cards at a team meeting and asking swimmers to write down their goals for the season. The necessity of writing goals forces swimmers to consider why they are participating in the program. The card, which is seen only by the coach, is a starting point for a one-on-one discussion with the swimmer.

With older swimmers, some of their goals should include the performance times the competitor wants to achieve at the end of the season. Meaningful goal times could be the cut-off time that qualifies swimmers to compete in a championship meet or the times that enabled swimmers to score points for their teams in the previous year's championship meet. For a talented swimmer, the club records may provide meaningful goal times. If possible, the swimmer should be the one to decide the goal time with prompting from the coach. A first-year swimmer's goal could be to race in each meet. The coach could associate this goal with the swimmer's perfecting techniques and attending every practice. Novice high school swimmers might state that their goals are to earn varsity letters. Early in the season, the coach could point out the times being achieved by teams the swimmers will soon compete against. The swimmers can then be asked their opinion of the times that will be necessary to gain points against these teams. These times will then become the swimmers' goal times. Next, the coach can refer to these goal times in practice with questions such as, "How close to your goal time was that swim?"

If the same novice swimmers have goal times that would qualify them as high school "All Americans," the coach should accept the unrealistic goals but point out that these are long-term goals that will require work over a period of years to be achieved. The coach can then suggest stepping stones to reach these long-term goals. The swimmers could be reminded of their current capabilities and then be asked to determine goal times that will serve as intermediate goals. The coach should also make a few remarks about the commitment necessary to achieve the long-term goals.

Swimmers 10 years of age and younger should not be expected to have the same kinds of goals as high school swimmers. Younger swimmers must place more emphasis on immediate goals because their performance next Saturday is more important to them than their performance in the championships 10 weeks away. Goals such as flipping every turn, holding the breath from the flags to the wall at the end of a swim, or being on time to every workout are examples of immediate goals that can be related to success at the next meet. A goal for this age group and for all swimmers should be to memorize their best times in their best events. In a meet, your swimmers should obtain their times from their timers immediately after finishing a race. They will then know immediately if they have improved their performance. Improving a "best time" is a realistic goal for this age group and one that is naturally fulfilled insofar as most swimmers 10 years of age or younger are growing in size and strength. It is possible for swimmers 10 years and under to improve a 50-yard time by 2 or 3 seconds each week. In comparison, older, more experienced swimmers might reduce their 50-yard time by only 2 or 3 seconds in a season.

In goal setting, the coach's role is to provide the information to allow swimmers to translate their goals into times that they can realistically achieve. The coach should accept all goals but should provide input to stimulate the most talented swimmers to consider difficult goals, whereas swimmers with less talent or commitment must also be made to realize that the goals they are pursuing are worthwhile.

Developing a Dryland Exercise Program

When surveyed, most coaches experienced with seasonal teams considered dryland exercise programs to be very important. Pool time is usually limited at this level, and young people respond best to a varied program. You will obtain the best results when flexibility, strength, and endurance exercises are done in 30-minute sessions three times each week under your direct supervision. This is most easily done before or after swimming practice. Your duties include preparing a list of the exercises before each meeting, checking that the exercises are done correctly, and ensuring that the athletes understand the purpose of the exercises.

The following eight basic concepts should be considered when organizing a dryland exercise program:

1. Dryland exercises should be done every other day so that muscles can rest and recover between sessions. Running may be substituted on alternate days to provide increased endurance.
2. Each exercise session and swimming session should be started with a warm-up. Flexibility exercises are used to stretch and warm up each section of the body.
3. Exercises should be specific. The specific muscles to be used in swimming should be exercised using the motions and rhythms that most nearly duplicate those used in the water.
4. A muscle should be worked more than normal if it is to become stronger. This is termed the overload principle.
5. To motivate swimmers, the coach should do the exercises with the swimmers whenever possible.
6. Increases in strength require 4 to 6 weeks of regular exercise. Swimmers should be told this and encouraged to be patient.
7. Power is the ability to do strength performances with speed. To develop power, some strength exercises should be performed hard and fast.
8. To be effective, exercises must be done correctly.

A comfortable compromise between variety and familiarity should be reached in your program. Performing exercises that have been done before is reassuring and all exercises should be done until they can easily be done correctly. Some new exercises should be presented at each session to prevent boredom. An excellent resource for further study is *Coaching Young Athletes* available through the American Coaching Effectiveness Program National Office, Box 5076, Champaign, IL 61820. The following suggestions for exercises are presented by categories to develop flexibility, strength, and endurance. Exercises that are suitable as warm-ups are designated with an asterisk (*).

Flexibility Exercises

Swimmers can get by with only average flexibility in the hip joint, but their flexibility in the ankles must be well above average for a strong kick (Counsilman, 1977). The freestyler and butterflyer need shoulder flexibility in order to recover their arms over the water easily. To improve flexibility, a muscle should be stretched slowly for 20 to 30 seconds. The stretch is then increased slightly just before the muscle is relaxed.

(7.1) For the Calf Muscle and Heel Cord
The swimmer gets into the track starting position with most of the body weight supported by the arms. The left knee is bent under the chest with the foot flat on the floor. Keeping the head up, the swimmer stretches the right leg back as far as possible. The heel should be gently stretched down for 15 seconds while keeping the right leg straight. The swimmer slides the leg back a few inches and holds as shown in Figure 7-1.

Fig. 7-1

(7.2) For the Calf Muscle and Heel Cord
The swimmer stands 2 to 3 feet from a wall with one foot 6 inches in front of the other. The palms of the hands are placed on the wall with the elbows straight. Keeping the back straight, the head in line with the body, and the feet flat on the floor, the swimmer bends the elbows as far as possible. Hold the position for 20 seconds and then increase the stretch before relaxing. Do this exercise twice, reversing the forward foot.

(7.3) For Ankle Stretch
In a straight-leg sitting position, the swimmer flexes the feet toward the legs. Tell your swimmers to hold for 20 seconds and to then extend the entire foot toward the floor, curling the toes downward. The swimmer then holds again for 20 seconds.

(7.4) For Lower Back and Back of the Legs Stretch
Swimmers sit on the floor with their legs straight, knees to the floor, and feet flat on the wall. Tell your swimmers to exhale and reach for the wall, keeping the knees to the floor and the feet in position. The swimmer should eventually touch the wall with a closed fist.

(7.5) For Lower Back and Inner Sides of the Thigh
Have your swimmers sit on the floor with the right leg in front and the left leg bent back with the inside of the ankle touching the floor. The swimmer tries to pull the head to the right knee by grasping the ankle and pulling with the arms (see Figure 7-2).

Fig. 7-2

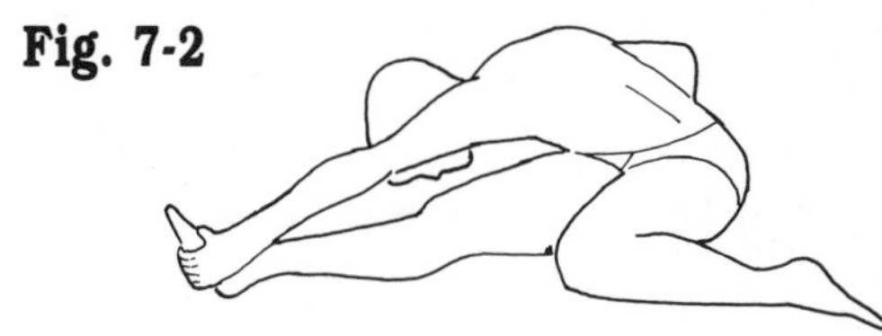

(7.6) For the Shoulder Joint
In a sitting position, tell your swimmers to roll both shoulders up, back, down, and around in a continuous movement. Follow this exercise

with the same motion with the right shoulder only and then with the left shoulder only.

(7.7) For the Shoulder Joint
Have your swimmers hold a towel behind the back. Tell them to lift the arms as high as possible, keeping the head up and the back straight. The swimmers hold this position for 20 seconds. Next the swimmers hold the towel over the head with the arms straight. Bend the elbows so that the towel is lowered behind the head down to the shoulders.

Strength Exercises

The types of strengthening exercises used by most recreational swimming coaches can be done without elaborate equipment. One type of strength exercise involves concentric muscle contractions. Concentric contraction occurs when a muscle shortens and contracts sufficiently to overcome a resistance. An example of this is moving from lying on the back to sitting up in the first phase of a sit-up. A second type of exercise involves eccentric contraction, the slow controlled lengthening of a contracting muscle. For instance, when the athlete doing the sit-up returns to the back lying position, the muscles work against gravity in an eccentric contraction to allow a controlled return. In both eccentric and concentric contractions, a part of the body actually moves.

In contrast, isometrics, another type of exercise, are done by contracting the muscle without motion against a stationary resistance. One precaution with using isometrics is that the exercise should be performed at several positions throughout the entire range of motion of the stroke. Since 1957 when Counsilman credited isometric exercises with developing strength while encouraging proper stroke mechanics, isometric exercises have been widely used to strengthen swimmers' muscles. Counsilman's favorite exercise was to have his swimmers pull over a barrel, thereby practicing the high elbow pull of the crawl stroke (Counsilman, 1977). (see Figure 7-3.)

Fig. 7-3

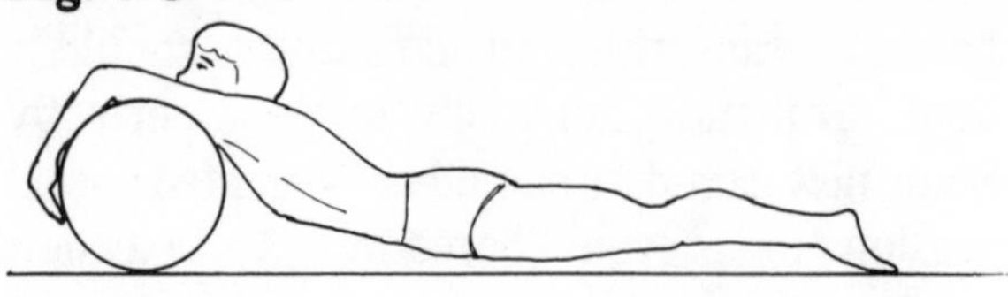

Isometric Exercises for Arm Strength

(7.8) For Butterflyers, Freestylers, and Backstrokers
The butterfly or freestyle swimmer stands, whereas the backstroke swimmer kneels. The backstroker pushes up while the partner pushes down. The elbows of both swimmers are kept high in the swimming position. Because recreational swimmers should not yet specialize in one stroke, have partners change positions at the completion of the exercise (see Figure 7-4).

Fig. 7-4

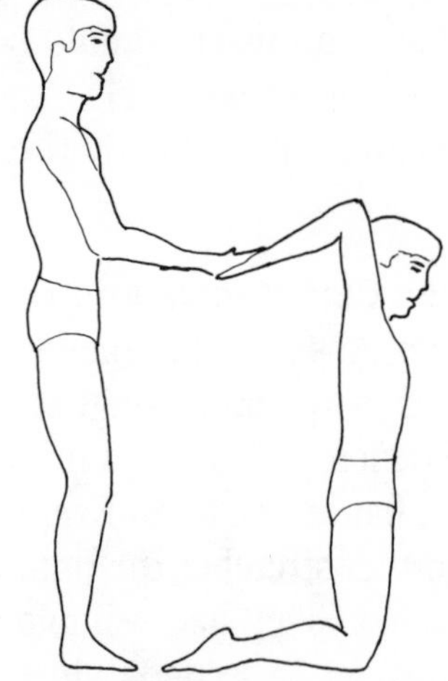

(7.9) For Breaststrokers
Two breaststrokers stand facing each other with their palms touching. Tell them to press against each other's hands as they pull backward with the elbows high. The partners change positions after a series of six repetitions and do three sets each (see Figure 7-5).

Fig. 7-5

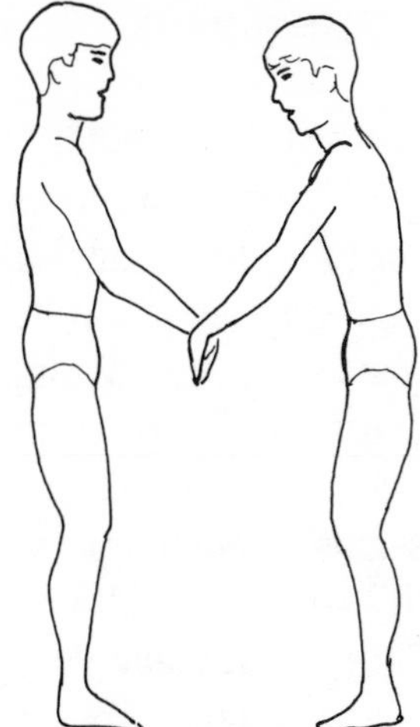

(7.10) For All Racing Strokes

Partners stand facing each other with their palms pressing against each other in an up-and-down action. One partner presses while the other resists to practice the press phase of the armstroke (see Figure 7-6).

Fig. 7-6

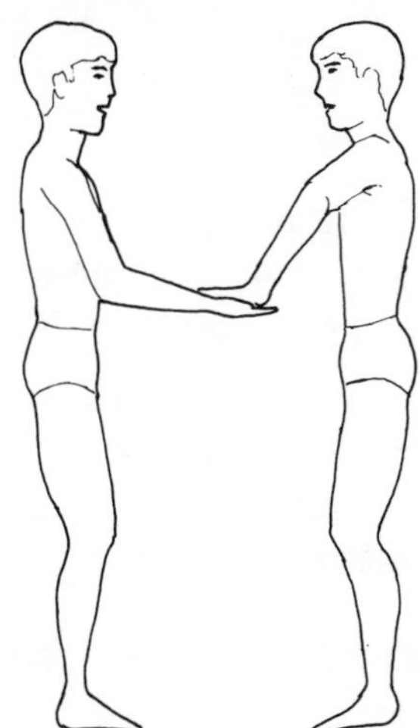

(7.11) For Butterflyers and Freestylers

The swimmer stands with the back 5 inches from the wall. The palms of both hands push against the wall. This action strengthens the follow-through action of the crawl and butterfly strokes (see Figure 7-7).

Fig. 7-7

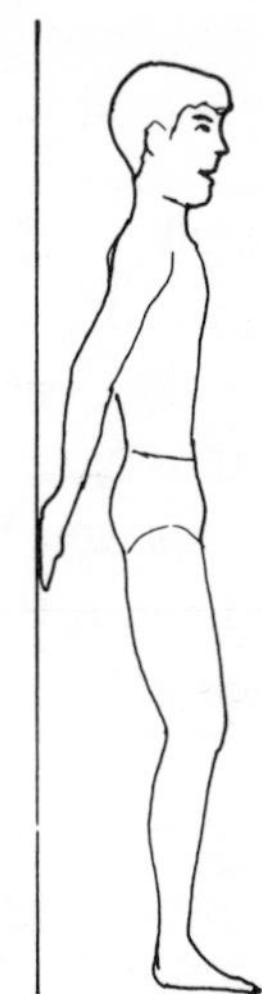

Concentric and Eccentric Exercises

(7.12) Abdominal Strength

1. The swimmer lies on the back with the hands clasped behind the neck. With the knees bent at a 90-degree angle, the swimmer rolls up and touches the elbows to the knees before returning to the original position (see Figures 7-8 and 7-9).

Fig. 7-8

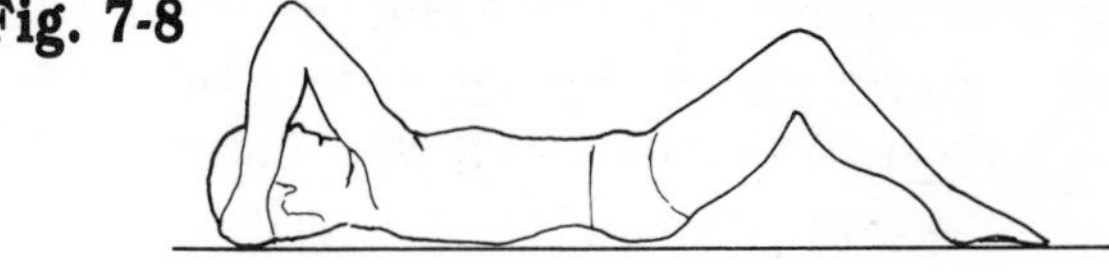

Fig. 7-9

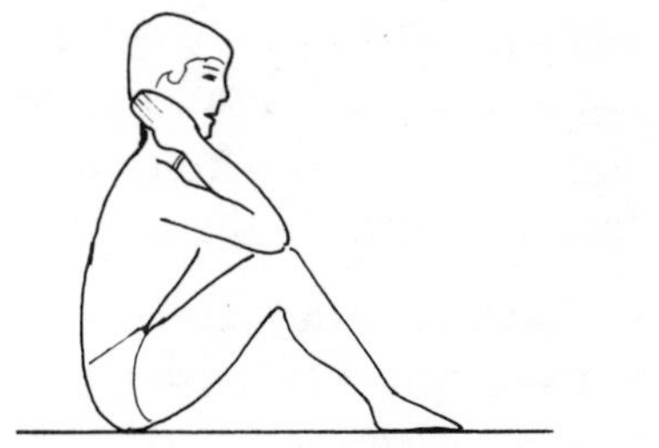

2. Use this exercise on days that you do not use Exercise 1. The swimmer starts as in Exercise 1 but may have a partner hold down the feet. The swimmer sits halfway up, then twists to the side with the whole trunk (not just the head and arms), and then returns to the starting position.
3. The swimmer again starts with the legs as they were in Exercise 1, but now the arms are at the sides. The swimmer lifts the knees to the chest, raising the hips off the floor. This is followed by a controlled return to the

starting position. Be sure that the swimmer keeps the knees bent.

(7.13) Arm Strength

1. Have your swimmers do traditional push-ups with the feet pointed and the weight on the tops of the feet. If swimmers cannot do the push-ups, have them hold the support position with the back flat for the time it takes teammates to do an assigned number.
2. Swimmers stand one and one half arm lengths from the wall. Tell them to lean forward and place the hands on the wall with the elbows straight. With the heels down, the swimmer bends the elbows until the nose touches the wall and then returns to the starting position. This exercise also gives a stretch through the ankles.

(7.14) Leg Strength

1. Have your swimmers jump in place, pointing the toes as much as possible and going as high as possible on each jump.
2. Swimmers stand facing a partner, holding right hands. The performer stands on the right foot and squats down, keeping the left leg straight and parallel to the floor. When the leg is 6 inches from the floor, the performer returns to the standing position

The above concentric and eccentric exercises can be used to increase power. To increase power, the exercises must be done with speed. When working with children under 12 years of age, some coaches repeat the exercises for the time it takes the swimmers to swim their best strokes for 25 yards. With children over 12 years of age, choose a time to correspond to swimming 50 yards of their best stroke. When the swimmer is able to increase the number of performances in the designated time by five repetitions, then the time for the drill is lengthened by 5 seconds. The drill is lengthened until the time span is equal to the best 50-yard time for swimmers under 12 years of age and the best 100-yard time for swimmers 12 or older.

Endurance Exercises

Endurance is the relative ability to continue exercising at a given rate of intensity for a specified length of time. Running 3 days each week has been suggested as a way to help improve cardiovascular endurance. Swimming itself is an aerobic activity that builds endurance. In addition, many recreational coaches conduct dryland exercise sessions on Mondays, Wednesdays, and Fridays with a run of about 25 minutes on Tuesdays and Thursdays. Have your swimmers do two of the following endurance exercises for approximately 5 minutes of each dryland exercise session during the midseason. Omit the endurance work during the late season because 2 days of running and regular swimming workouts will maintain your athletes' endurance at this time.

(7.15) Running in Place

In this exercise the swimmers point their toes as they run in place to prepare for good push-offs from turns and the pointed toes used in the flutter kick.

(7.16) Crawl Stroking Out of Water

Crawl stroking while standing in place may be timed by a watch or pace clock. Choose the time that it takes most of your athletes to swim 200 yards and assign the exercise for that length of time. Emphasize to your swimmers the importance of maintaining proper stroke techniques.

(7.17) Running in Place While Doing the Crawl Stroke

Use this exercise on days that you do not use Exercise 1 or 2. Count three runs for each stroke.

(7.18) Crawl Kicking

Swimmers lie prone with the arms down by the sides and under them and the palms of the hands supporting the thighs. They then kick up vigorously with small kicks as in the crawl stroke.

(7.19) Sitting Flutter Kicks

Use this exercise on days that you do not use the crawl kicking (7.18). Swimmers sit on the back of the hips with their hands on their hips and their legs off the floor. They then whip the legs up and down with loose ankles at a rate of 240 per minute, exhaling on the first three kicks and inhaling on the next three.

Before the First Workout

Swimming workouts will go smoothly if team members understand (a) how to swim in circles, (b) how to read a pace clock, and (c) how to take a carotid pulse before their first workout.

Circle Swimming

Use a blackboard to diagram circle swimming as shown in Figure 7-10. Explain that in Lane 1

Fig. 7-10

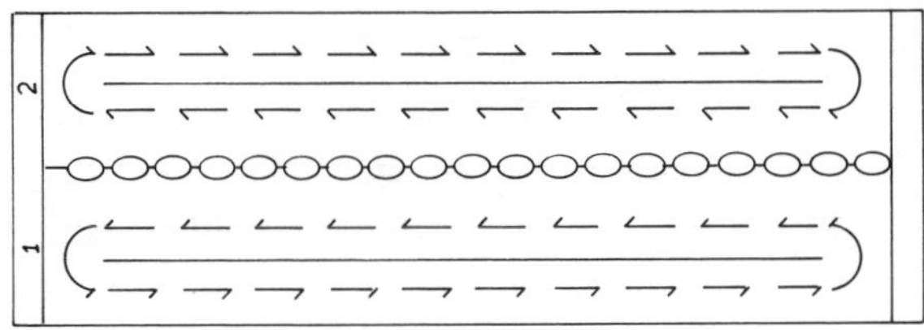

each competitor swims down the right side of the lane. A cut to the left is made just before the turn so that the streamlined push-off from the flip turn is made on the correct side of the lane. The swimmers are then again on their own right side. If one swimmer overtakes another swimmer and wants to pass, the passer taps the foot of the overtaken swimmer. On the next turn, the overtaken swimmer swims to the far corner of the lane and holds the wall for a moment, thus allowing the swimmer who is passing to flip the turn toward the center of the lane and push off on the right in front of the overtaken swimmer.

The swimmers in Lane 2 of the diagram are swimming in a clockwise circle. This avoids bumping or hitting with the recovery arm because swimmers in adjoining lanes are always going in the same direction. Swimmers in all odd-numbered lanes will circle in the same direction as those in Lane 1. All swimmers in the even-numbered lanes will circle in the same direction as shown in Lane 2 in Figure 7-10.

Reading a Pace Clock

Explain to your swimmers that the pace clock will run continuously during practice. Point out that one hand of the clock goes around every 60 seconds. The other hand moves only one small line each minute (see Figure 7-11).

Fig. 7-11

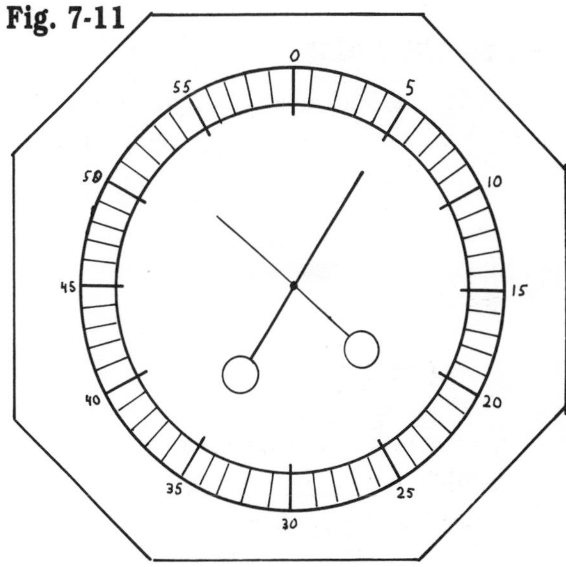

If a swimmer is swimming a set of ten 50-yard swims (10 × 50) on an assigned swimming time of 1 minute, the swimmer would leave on the same clock number each interval. If that number is 0 and the swimmer takes 40 seconds to swim 50 yards, the swimmer finishes on the 40, rests for 20 seconds, and starts again on the 0. For example, this is indicated as 4 × 50 on 1:00 in the practice plans provided.

Ask the swimmers to imagine that they are swimming a set of 5 × 100 yards on a swimming time of 1:30 and that their average time for swimming 100 yards is 1:20. If they start their first 100-yard swim on the 0, they will get 10 seconds of rest before starting their second 100-yard swim on the 30 and their third on the 0. When they understand this, give other examples such as the following for your swimmers to interpret. Swimmers are going to swim 12 × 25 yards on the :45 (i.e., departure time of 45 seconds). They start on the 0 and take 30 seconds to swim 25 yards. How much rest will they get and on what number will they start their second, third, and fourth 25-yard swims? Explain that swimmers will leave one at a time, 5 seconds behind the person in front of them so that if the first swimmer in a lane leaves on 0, the second will leave when the hand of the clock is on 5 and the third will leave on 10.

Taking the Pulse

To find the carotid pulse, swimmers place the index or middle finger on the carotid artery beside the windpipe and under the jaw (see Figure 7-12).

Fig. 7-12

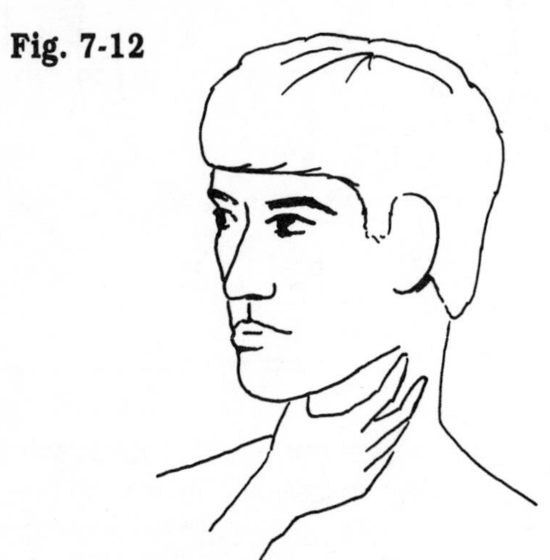

Have your swimmers take the pulse for 6 seconds and multiply the result by 10 to determine the pulse rate per minute. Resting pulse rates (the rate when the body is at rest) in children vary but can be expected to be slightly faster than the 72 normal pulse rate in adults and persons in their late teens. Following an all-out 2-minute swim, the pulse rate will be 180 to 200 beats per minute regardless of the resting pulse rate. A very easy 2-minute swim should bring the pulse rate to around 110 (Counsilman, 1979). As the swimmer's cardiovascular condition improves, the pulse rate on the easy swim should become lower. Thus the pulse can be used as a diagnostic tool to determine how hard a swimmer is working on a particular phase of the workout.

Elements of Early Season Workouts

Early season workouts for swimmers over 10 years of age should contain the following elements:

- *Stretching period*

Approximately 10 minutes should be designated for stretching on dry land before each workout and before meet warm-ups. Use the flexibility exercises listed earlier in this manual.

- *Warm-up*

A distance swim without concern for the time, usually 200 to 400 yards of the crawl stroke, should be included. Other racing strokes may be done, but the butterfly is never done until the swimmer has warmed up.

- *Stroke work*

During the early season, each workout should include group work on a specific stroke or skill. Later in the season, stroke work is done on an individual basis.

- *Interval training*

In interval training, a certain distance is swum and followed by a rest. Swimmers repeat this cycle a specified number of times within a given time frame. This may be given to the swimmers as "5 × 50 on 1 minute," if you know the swimmers take approximately 40 seconds to swim 50 yards and will have 20 seconds to rest. If you are unsure of times, the interval training could be given as 5 × *50 with 20-second rests.* The stroke to be used is specified to the swimmers, as well as the quality of the swim they are to perform. The following phrases describe the quality of the swim:

Medium speed
Second length harder than the first
Every other 50 hard
Every other 50 within 10 seconds of your best time

Keep every 50 under 40 seconds
Try to raise your pulse rate above 150

Keep in mind that longer rests are used when quality swims are required and shorter rests are used for swims of less expected quality. However, when using interval training, allow the swimmer to rest only partially rather than completely.

• *Repetition training*
Repetition training includes sprinting and may include hypoxic work. It is done with enough rest to allow the pulse rate to return to under 100 beats per minute between each effort. Repetition training includes work in all the strokes.

As listed, the stretching and warm-up elements of a workout are always given first; the interval swimming and kicking may be given in either order in the middle; and the repetition training is usually given at the end. A period of stroke work should also be included in each early season workout. This is easily incorporated into the interval training portion of the workout. Workouts for swimmers 10 years of age and under should contain the previously listed elements but with shorter distances and more time spent on the kicking sets and stroke work. A game, race, or relay should be included at the end of each workout for swimmers 10 and under.

Sample Early Season Workouts

Sample Workout 1

Swimmers: Recreational swimmers 10 years of age and under
Time in the water: Approximately 55 minutes
Yards swum: 700
Objectives: To show that workouts are fun
To review the crawl stroke
To introduce racing

Organization: Entire workout is done using the *width* of the pool.

Warm-Up: Swim 8 widths with your best stroke, go across easy, swim back at medium speed, rest 5 seconds each width. The coach uses the rest time to make comments to the swimmers.

Kicking: 16 widths of crawl kicking on :50. Make group suggestions during the rest period.

Stroke Work: In waist-deep water, with feet on the bottom, practice crawl armstroke with breathing. Demonstrate in the water with swimmers. Bend over so water is at bathing cap level on head. Do 4 sets of 20 strokes with 10-second rest after each set.

Interval Work: 10 widths of armstroke pulling drill with kickboard; 10-second rest between each width.
10 widths of entire stroke on :30. Again make group comments during rest.

Stroke Work: Teach and practice grab start from the side.

Repetition Work: Divide swimmers into relay teams of no more than 4 swimmers each. Run 4 relays. For one relay, kick across the pool with boards and pass the board to a teammate. All swimmers start in the water. For the second relay, use the arms alone, and then two relays using the crawl stroke.

Sample Workout 2

Swimmers:	Recreational swimmers 10 years of age and under
Time in the Water:	Approximately 65 minutes
Yards Swum:	1,150
Objectives:	To review the breaststroke To teach and practice the underwater stroke
Warm-Up: 1 × 200 crawl	5 seconds of rest after each length. Use this rest to keep swimmers thinking about their stroke.
Kicking: 4 × 50 kick on 1:30	Using flutter boards, flutter kick down the pool and breaststroke kick back.
Stroke Work: 4 ×25	Combine armstroke and kick for breaststroke on return. Review the number on the pace clock when they will leave.
Underwater Stroke:	Teach first from a push-off, then from a dive.
Interval Work: 4 × 50 swim on 1:30	Backstroke down and breaststroke back. Use the underwater stroke between back and breast.
Interval Work: 4 × 50 swim on 1:30	Breaststroke down and crawl stroke back. Start each 50 with underwater stroke.
Repetition Work: 10 × 25 swim	On command, first length, swimmers push off from wall, do underwater stroke, and swim breaststroke for pool length. On return lengths, swimmers dive in, rather than push from wall and do underwater stroke. Anyone forgetting the underwater stroke does gutter push-ups.

Sample Workout 3

Swimmers:	Recreational swimmers 10 years of age and under
Time in the Water:	Approximately 50 minutes
Yards Swum:	Approximately 1,000
Objectives:	To present the butterfly To review the breaststroke and crawl To practice breath control
Stroke Work:	Mirror Drill
Warm-Up: 1 × 150 swim	Crawl on odd lengths and breaststroke on even.
Kicking: 10 × 25 kick on :45	Use butterfly kick first 5 lengths with a board and last 5 lengths without a board.
Interval Work: 2 × 50 drill :20 rest	Butterfly drill with kickboard.
10 × 25 drill on :20 rest	Butterfly drill using left arm, right arm, both arms.
Repetition Work: 4 × 25 swim	On *Go* command, ½ length butterfly, ½ length freestyle.
Interval Work:	Sharks and Minnows. Coach or 1 swimmer who is "it" starts as a shark by treading water in the middle of the pool. All others are minnows on the side of the pool. On command, minnows swim to the other side of the pool without being tagged. All tagged players become sharks and help tag minnows the next time across. Minnows can only be tagged at the surface, but sharks can lift minnows to the surface. The last minnow tagged is the winner. Any time there is contact in the water, there must be a safety signal, such as a pinch to signal that the minnow gives up and will become a shark.

Sample Workout 4

Swimmers:	Recreational swimmers over 10 years of age
Time in the Water:	Approximately 1 hour, 15 minutes
Yards Swum:	1,600
Objectives:	To show that workouts are fun To survey the talent To introduce circle swimming
Organization:	Divide the number of swimmers by the number of lanes in the pool. On land, arrange the swimmers in a line according to height. If you have 30 swimmers in a 6-lane pool, put the tallest 5 in the first lane with the tallest swimmer leading the lane, the second 5 in the second lane, etc. As they swim the first 200 yards, rearrange the swimmers who are clearly too slow for their lanes. When your team swims lengths from a dive take swimmers out of the water and rearrange them so that your fastest swimmers (Lane 1) are swimming against each other, side by side, instead of behind each other.
Warm-Up: 200 crawl	One length easy and the next length medium speed. Concentrate on staying to the right of the lane.
Kicking: 20 × 25 kick on :45	Kick with the face above water. Help swimmers to leave on the correct interval.
Stroke Work: 1 × 25 duck drill	Explain need for high elbows both above and under the water. Then try drill. Leave on command.
Stroke Work: 1 × 25 modified duck drill	On command.
Interval Work: 4 × 25	Use one arm going down the pool and the other coming back. Emphasize pulling past the bathing suit. Leave on command.
Interval Work: 8 × 25 on :45	Arms alone.
Repetition: 6 ×50	Take pulse after each 50. When pulse is below 10 for 6 seconds, do the next 50 all-out.
Repetition: 10 × 25 crawl	Do on command from a dive if air is not too cold.

Sample Workout 5

Swimmers:	Swimmers over 10 years of age
Time in the Water:	Approximately 1 hour, 15 minutes
Yards swum:	2,050
Objectives:	To strengthen kick To review breaststroke To review underwater stroke To improve hypoxic work
Warm-Up: Locomotive 300	1 length is done slowly, 1 length fast; then 2 lengths slowly, 2 lengths fast; finally, 3 lengths slowly, 3 lengths fast.
Kicking: 4 × 75 on 2:00	Use boards. For first 75, 50 fly, 25 breast. For second 75, 50 back, 25 breast. For third 75, 75 breast. For fourth 75, 50 crawl, 25 breast.
Stroke Work: Breaststroke Turn	Review or teach underwater stroke off walls. Have a contest to see who can push off underwater and swim the farthest with a legal underwater stroke. Emphasize streamlined position.
Interval Work: 8 × 100 with :20 rest	20-second rest between each 100. 50 breast, 50 crawl. Emphasize touching with 2 hands on the turn.
Hypoxic Work: 1 × 500	Crawl. Every third length, take 4 breaths per length.
Repetition Work: 6 × 25 relays	3 relay races of breaststroke, 1 each of other strokes.
Organization:	Relays may be made quickly as in the first workout. Half the swimmers go to the other end for 25-yard relays.

Sample Workout 6

Swimmers:	Swimmers over 10 years of age
Time in the Water:	Approximately 1 hour, 15 minutes
Yards Swum:	2,050
Objectives:	To review all 4 racing strokes To introduce transitions for the individual medley
Warm-Up: 1 × 300	Crawl stroke; 2 lengths easy, 1 length hard.
Kicking: 1 × 400	(IM) individual medley kick using boards for all strokes except backstroke.
Stroke Work: 12 yards × 20	Explain the techniques for changing from butterfly to backstroke and from breaststroke to crawl. Practice these from 6 yards away from the turn. These transitions are done efficiently by many swimmers naturally, but unless they have been tried in practice, many swimmers will forget to streamline when pushing off the walls.
Interval Work: 5 × 50 on 1:30	Fly, back.
5 × 50 on 1:30	Back, breast.
5 × 50 on 1:30	Breast, crawl.
4 × 100 on 3:00	Individual medley.
Repetition: 8 × 25	On *Go* command from a dive. Do strokes in IM order, swim to end of pool, do transition, and then get out of the water.

Evaluating Your Progress

1. Name three ways you can help your swimmers to formulate appropriate goals.
2. What is your response to a goal that is too difficult for a swimmer? A goal that is too easy?
3. Name three duties of the coach of a dryland exercise session.
4. Without referring to the text, name as many basic concepts as possible that you must adhere to in a dryland exercise program.
5. How can coaches who want to improve their swimmers' power adjust strengthening exercises?
6. The swimmers in your program lack endurance. Which adjustments to your dryland exercise program will increase their endurance levels?

   a. Do vigorous exercises rapidly.
   b. Do vigorous exercises for 5 minutes or longer.
   c. Do exercises that stretch the muscles.

7. To improve flexibility, a muscle should be stretched

   a. 2-3 seconds
   b. 20-30 seconds
   c. One minute or longer

8. The swimmers in your program have doubled the number of sit-ups and push-ups they can do, but their power while swimming has not shown a marked increase. How should you adjust their strengthening exercises to increase their power?

   a. Encourage swimmers to further increase the number of sit-ups and push-ups they can do.
   b. Encourage swimmers to do the same number of sit-ups and push-ups but to do them faster.
   c. Encourage swimmers to stretch for a longer period of time before swimming.

9. The swimmers in your program are not getting a strong push-off from the walls on their starts and turns. List some dryland exercises that would improve their abilities in this area.
10. List three rules that swimmers must observe to circle swim successfully.
11. What is the expected pulse rate following an all-out 2-minute swim?

    a. 70-80
    b. 120-130
    c 180-200

12. List the five elements of an early season workout.

Chapter 8: Midseason Training

At the conclusion of this chapter, you should be prepared to employ correct information for the following midseason coaching tasks:

- Increasing your swimmers' endurance through proper and interesting workouts.
- Adjusting workouts to various ability levels.
- Improving your swimmers' racing techniques.
- Creating an atmosphere of enthusiasm and team spirit among your swimmers.

Increasing Endurance

By midseason your swimmers will have been exposed to proper strokes, proper turns, and proper starting techniques. Workouts given during midseason will still be directed toward perfecting these skills, but more time will be spent on individual correction than on group drills. Practice time during midseason is devoted to work on *endurance* swimming. Muscular endurance is the ability of muscles to continue to make specific movements without tiring. If your competitors can swim 25 yards fast but have trouble finishing a 200-yard swim, they lack endurance. Endurance is increased by repeating a specific movement many times.

The longest workouts, those of 3,000 to 4,000 yards, will be given during midseason, and approximately 70% of the yards swum will be spent on interval training. In interval training, swimmers could be assigned ten 200-yard swims with only 10 seconds of rest between each 200 yards, and by repeating the muscle contraction many times, the swimmer's endurance is increased.

One challenge for you as a coach is to keep endurance workouts from being boring. A few techniques used by coaches to increase interest include the following:

- Never repeat a workout.
- Don't tell swimmers what the workout will be until they arrive at practice and then describe and conduct only one set at a time. You will find your swimmers trying to outguess each other about what comes next and generally enjoying the surprise.
- Keep your swimmers thinking about the workout by giving special instructions for each swim such as the following:
  1. Sprint the even lengths.
  2. Swim a negative split. (In a 100-yard swim, the second 50-yard length is swum faster than the first 50 yards.)
  3. Try to use ten strokes per length.
  4. Take eight breaths on the odd-numbered lengths.
- Vary the strokes by including each racing stroke in every workout.
- Celebrate swimmers' birthdays or achievements by designing a workout of their favorite sets.
- Play games to determine what you will do. For example, have a swimmer throw dice or draw cards to determine the stroke or distance to be swum.

- Use your imagination to contrive new races such as 125-yard individual medleys (one 25-yard length each of the crawl, butterfly, backstroke, breaststroke, and repeat crawl) or backward 100-yard individual medleys (one 25-yard length each of the crawl, breaststroke, backstroke, and butterfly).
- Following a warm-up, assign a different skill to swimmers in each lane. List the skills on the blackboard. As soon as swimmers complete the workout for their lane, they move to the next lane, where they complete the skill assigned for that lane as in the following example:

Lane 1	5 × 100	Crawl armstroke with 10 seconds of rest after each 100 yards. Breathe every third stroke.
Lane 2	8 × 50	Flutter kick on 1:30, negative split.
Lane 3	1 × 600	Crawl, every third length breaststroke.
Lane 4	10 × 50	Swim on 1:15. Odd 50s, butterfly backstroke; even 50s, breaststroke crawl.
Lane 5	15 × 25	Crawl on :40. Descend your times from the first to the third. (If you do the first 25 yards in 30 seconds, aim to do the next in 25 seconds, and the third in 20 seconds. Do this again on the fourth through the sixth seventh through ninth, etc.)
Lane 6	6 × 75	Pull, kick, and swim. For the first length, use arms alone. For the second length, kick. For the last length, use the whole stroke.

In this workout, all intervals must be easy enough for everyone to make. If you use harder intervals, tell anyone not making an interval to stop, add 5 seconds to the regular interval, and then try again.

- Develop a timed race termed a "monster." Swimmers start 5 seconds behind each other using a pace clock. The faster swimmers start first. Monsters may include the following:
  A. Exercises such as jumping jacks, push-ups, pull-ups, sit-ups, or gutter push-ups.
  B. Swimming all four racing strokes.
  C. Obstacle courses either on land or in the water. The course can require swimmers to go either over or under chairs, hoops, benches, poles, and other obstacles.
  D. Retrieving objects from the bottom of the pool.
  E. Diving off the board.
  F. A designated number of racing dives or turns.

Each swimmer receives a personal time for the monster. The fastest time in each age group should be posted with the swimmer's name. If you repeat the monster every week or month, you may also post the names of the most improved swimmers. Before presenting it to your team, try the monster yourself to check each stunt for safety.

Adjusting Workouts for a Wide Range of Abilities

Because recreational teams include every swimmer who is willing to attend practice, the coach is faced with the need to design meaningful endurance workouts for swimmers of varying abilities. During the early season, swimmers were assigned to lanes with other swimmers of similar speed. It becomes more important during midseason that swimmers always report to their assigned lanes. Although swimmers are grouped to work according to speed, you want all competitors to feel that they are part of the same team, with the same goals, and with their heads above water at the same time. The following adjustments will help all of your swimmers to identify with and feel part of the team:

- Allow swimmers in some lanes to rest during a specific part of the set as follows:

  12 × 50 yards on 1:00 freestyle
  Lane 1 & 2 Do all 12 × 50.
  Lane 3 Sit out every sixth 50.
  Lane 4 Sit out every fifth 50.
  Lane 5 Sit out every fourth 50.
  Lane 6 Sit out every third 50.

- Assign different intervals so that swimmers in the slower lanes have more time to accomplish the distance.

  12 × 50 yards freestyle
  Lanes 1 & 2 Do 12 × 50 on 1:00.
  Lane 3 Do 11 × 50 on 1:05.
  Lane 4 Do 10 × 50 on 1:10.
  Lane 5 Do 9 × 50 on 1:15.
  Lane 6 Do 8 × 50 on 1:20.

- Change to a slower stroke for the fastest swimmers.

  12 × 50 on 1:30
  Lanes 1 & 2 Do all 12 backstroke.
  Lanes 3 & 4 Alternate. Do one length backstroke, one length freestyle.
  Lane 5 & 6 Do all 12 freestyle.

- Maintain the same interval for all lanes but give the faster swimmers a longer distance on each interval.

  12 swims freestyle on 1:30
  Lanes 1 & 2 Do 12 × 75 on 1:30.
  Lanes 3 & 4 Do 12 × 50 on 1:30.
  Lanes 5 & 6 Do 12 × 25 and five gutter push-ups on 1:30.

Other suggestions include the following. When there are fewer than four swimmers in each lane, instruct any swimmer who cannot make the assigned interval to stop and begin on an interval 5 seconds slower. This way the swimmers will not interfere with each other. In distance swims, the coach may assign fewer lengths to the slower swimmers or, if more convenient, give distance swims by assigning a time and asking swimmers to see how many lengths they can accomplish in the given time.

Midseason Technique Work

Techniques and strokes are best perfected by practicing correctly. Swimmers who do not practice correctly usually have one of the following problems:

- *Misunderstanding the desired technique.* This problem is corrected by individually reviewing the skill you have taught either during or directly after practice. If the whole team cannot do a particular skill, then reteach the skill to the entire group.
- *Lack of concentration leading to sloppiness.* This problem results because practicing swimming can be boring. The head is in the water; there is nothing to look at except the black line on the bottom of the pool; and hearing reminders and corrections is difficult when the head is underwater.

The coach has three duties to perform in order to keep swimmers practicing correctly.

1. Set standards of correct practice and ensure that all swimmers understand them. Give your swimmers the following instructions at every practice:
   - Use legal, efficient strokes.
   - Use legal turns.
   - Streamline off the walls when turning or starting.
   - Finish each freestyle or butterfly set by keeping the face in the water from the flags to the wall.
   - Hit each finish hard.
2. Devise challenging workouts to hold your swimmers' interest.
3. Be alert to swimmers who are suffering a loss of concentration either because they are too tired or too bored. Adjust their workout to help regain their concentration.

Swimmers who maintain high practice standards will develop a positive self-image. They will not only have pride in themselves and their team, but they will also swim faster because they will use correct racing techniques automatically when they compete.

Coaches who demand high standards from their teams must have confidence in themselves, their coaching ability, and their teams. They must be sincerely interested in their swimmers. A good coach speaks to each swimmer individually at least once at each practice session. If the swimmer needs a reminder about stroke, you should provide this information. Questions such as "How did that feel?" "How close to your goal time was that?" or, to a swimmer who is not working hard, "Are you okay?" will let the swimmer know that you consider the workout important and the swimmer an important part of the team.

Coaches should show interest in their swimmers by providing for their comfort. Ideal water temperatures are 78 and 80 degrees Fahrenheit, and ideal air temperatures are 4 degrees above the water temperature. Coaches may be unable to change water and air conditions, but they can make the following workout adjustments to enhance their swimmers' comfort:

- If the water is cold, give shorter rests between sets and keep the swimmers moving.
- If the air is cold, raise the water temperature if possible.
- If both the air and water are cold, keep your swimmers in the water and moving. Evaporation requires heat, and getting swimmers in and out of the water will deplete the heat from their bodies.
- If the water is too warm, give fewer all-out efforts and more long swims.

Motivation and Team Spirit During Midseason

The greatest motivational factor for seasonal competitive swimmers is a good coach who displays enthusiasm and a positive attitude. Your attitude becomes especially important during midseason. In order to emphasize the importance of a coach's positive attitude, Robert F. Singer, a leading physical educator, divided students into four groups. Each group was given the same problems to solve. One group was put in a room with an instructor who offered only praise, another with an instructor who offered criticism, a third with an instructor who ignored the group, and the fourth in a room with no instructor. The group exposed to praise was most successful in their problem solving; the group exposed to criticism was second most successful. The group that was ignored ranked third in problem solving but did better than the group with no instructor present. This study demonstrates the importance of your attitude when coaching.

Coaches often ask, "How can I have a positive attitude when a swimmer has swum poorly?" The answer is that you must treat every mistake as a temporary setback. Tell your poor performer not to focus on past mistakes but rather on what will be done right the next time. Another important point is that you should praise a solid effort. Don't wait for the great performance to praise a swimmer's effort.

To maintain a positive attitude while making stroke corrections, you should first identify something that the swimmer is doing correctly. Let the swimmer know about this and then add the simple adjustment to make this correct attribute even more effective. The following additional motivational strategies will help you to establish and convey a positive attitude:

- *Getting parents and friends to attend meets*
  1. Have meet schedules available for anyone showing interest.
  2. List the names of the swimmers and their achievements on the schedules.
  3. Use bulletin boards, newspapers, and loudspeaker announcements to publicize meets.

4. Hold meets that honor alumni to keep former swimmers involved in your program.
   A short student/alumni relay may be one of the highlights of this meet.

- *Give swimmers status and a sense of belonging to a team*
  1. Display trophies, team pictures, and a team record board in a prominent place.
  2. Do things together as a team. Hold a picnic or attend a school or professional sporting event as a team. Spontaneous get-togethers work well, but a date for at least one event should be set early in the season to ensure maximum participation.
  3. Encourage use of uniform team caps, suits, or tee shirts.
  4. Prominently display a team banner at meets.
- *Let your swimmers know that you care about the team and each individual on the team*
  1. Be consistent and fair to each swimmer.
  2. Enjoy practice and make practice enjoyable for your swimmers.
  3. Talk to each swimmer at every workout.
  4. Start practice sessions on time.
  5. Spend the practice time with your swimmers, not in the office, on the phone, or talking with parents.
  6. Know each swimmer's interests and future plans.
  7. Call a swimmer who is sick or injured.

Sample Midseason Workouts

Sample Workout 1

Swimmers:	Recreational swimmers 10 years of age and under
Time in the water:	Approximately 70 minutes
Yards swum:	2,150
Objectives:	To increase endurance To work on all strokes for the individual medley To review the transition from backstroke to breaststroke
Warm-Up: 4 × 100 with :10 rest	Crawl, back, breast, and crawl.
Kicking: 12 × 50 on 1:20	Kick 1 × 50 of each stroke in the order of the individual medley and then repeat 3 times.
Interval Work: 4 × 125 with :30 rest	Crawl, break 5 seconds after each 25 yards.
8 × 50 on 1:30	Back, breast. Try to have a pulse over 150 after each 50 yards.
Repetition: 10 × 25	On *Go* command from a dive, first 12 ½ yards butterfly; last 12 ½ yards easy crawl.

Sample Workout 2

Swimmers:	Recreational swimmers 10 years of age and under
Time in the water:	Approximately 75 minutes
Yards swum:	2,350
Objectives:	To increase endurance To work on all strokes
Warm-Up: 6 × 75 with :10 rest	2 lengths swimmer's choice stroke. 1 length crawl with only 6 breaths.
Kicking: 20 × 25 on :45	Swimmer's choice of kick. Use boards.
Interval Work: 4 × 75 with :20 rest	Alternate 1 length each of back, breast, and crawl. Repeat 4 times.
3 × 100 with :20 rest	1 × 100 of breast, 1 × 100 of back, 1 × 100 of crawl.
6 × 50 with :20 rest	2 × 50 back, 2 × 50 breast, 2 × 50 crawl.
12 × 25 with :20 rest	4 × 25 breast, 4 × 25 back, 4 × 25 crawl.
Repetition Work: 8 × 25 relays	2 × 25 of ½ length fly; ½ length crawl; 2 × 25 breast; 2 × 25 back; 2 × 25 crawl.

Sample Workout 3

Swimmers:	Recreational swimmers 10 years of age and under
Time in the water:	70 minutes
Yards swum:	2,200
Objectives:	To keep swimmers interested and thinking To improve endurance To review all strokes To have fun
Warm-Up: 1 × 300 with :05 rest	Rest after each 25 yd length. Change strokes every third length.
Kicking: 16 × 25 with 10 seconds rest	IM-order fly and backstroke without a board, free and breast with a board.
Interval Work: 20 × 50 on 1:15	½ length fly, ½ length back, ½ length breast, ½ length free. Pick a mark or run a rope to designate halfway point on pool.
Repetition Work: 20 × 25	Swimmers leave on *Go* command from a dive. First swimmer done in each heat draws from a deck of playing cards to determine next stroke for his or her heat. Clubs-fly, Diamonds-back, Hearts-breast, Spades-Fly.

Sample Workout 4

Swimmers:	Recreational swimmers over 10 years of age
Time in the water:	Approximately 85 minutes
Yards swum:	3,525
Objectives:	To improve endurance To increase awareness of times To review all strokes in the IM To practice swimming at race pace
Warm-Up: 10 × 75 yd with :10 rest	1 length crawl, 1 length swimmer's choice, 1 length crawl (crawl, choice, crawl).
Kicking: 20 × 25 yd on :30	Swimmer's choice of kick.
Interval Work: 400 yd with :30 rest	"On the way" get the time of the first 200 yards (split).
200 yd with :30 rest	Swim faster than the first split of the 400. Get the 100 split "on the way."
100 yd with :30 rest	Swim faster than the first split of the 200. Get the 50 split "on the way."
50 yd with :30 rest	Swim faster than the first 50 yd split of the 100. Get the 25 split "on the way."
25 yd	Swim faster than the first split of the 50. Remember your time.
10 × 125 yd on 2:30	Crawl, butterfly, backstroke, breaststroke, crawl.
Repetition Work: 10 × 25 yd on 1:00	Keep times faster than last 25 split of the "on the way."

Sample Workout 5

Swimmers:	Recreational swimmers over 10 years of age
Time in the water:	Approximately 95 minutes
Yards swum:	3,375
Objectives:	To build endurance To work on all strokes
Warm-Up: 1 × 600	Swim first 3 lengths crawl, change stroke every third length thereafter.
Kicking: 8 × 50 on 1:10	Crawl kick on first length, swimmer's choice on second length.
Interval Work: 15 × 75 with :10 rest	Pull, kick, swim. On 25 pull arms alone, 25 kick legs only, 25 swim whole stroke.
10 × 100 on 2:30	Odd 100s freestyle, even 100s individual medley. Take your pulse after the individual medleys and try to have it at least 180.
Repetition Work: 10 × 25 on 1:00	Swim first 12 ½ yards hard with no breathing. Swim second half of length easy.

Sample Workout 6

Swimmers:	Recreational swimmers over 10 years of age
Time in the water:	Approximately 85 minutes
Yards swum:	3,350
Objectives:	To improve endurance To review strokes To have fun
Warm-Up: Freestyle locomotive up to 4 and back down again	In a locomotive, swimmer does 1 length slow and 1 length fast and then 2 lengths slow and 2 lengths fast. In this case swim up to 4 slow and 4 fast. The swimmer repeats 4 and works back down to 1 slow and 1 fast.
Kicking: 10 × 75 on 1:30	Free, breast, free.
Interval Work: 12 × 100 on 2:00	50 free, 50 fly. 50 free, 50 back. 50 free, 50 breast. 50 free, 50 free.
Repetition Work: 12 × 25 relay race	Each relay swimmer does each stroke 3 times in relay order.

Evaluating Your Progress

1. How many yards are included for those over 10 years of age in a recreational team's endurance workout during midseason?
   a. 1,000-2,000 yards
   b. 2,000-3,000 yards
   c. 3,000-4,000 yards
   d. 4,000-5,000 yards
2. What type of training is stressed in a midseason workout?
   a. Repetition work
   b. Interval work
   c. Stroke work
3. List at least five techniques a coach can use during midseason to keep workouts interesting.
4. List at least four ways a coach can adjust a workout so that all swimmers are stopped at the same time.
5. List your own standards for an efficient practice.
6. List three ways to get spectators to attend a meet.

Chapter 9: Late Season Training

At the conclusion of this chapter, you should be prepared to employ correct information for the following late season and taper tasks:

- Introducing techniques that will develop your swimmers' sense of pace.
- Creating workouts appropriate for swimmers in late season and taper training.
- Presenting challenges to your team that will help them adjust to the stress of championship meets.
- Helping swimmers prepare to swim their fastest times.
- Establishing an exciting yet enjoyable atmosphere prior to the most important meet of the season.

Establishing a Sense of Pace

The emphasis during the late season is on swimming fast and establishing and maintaining a desirable pace. Swimmers must develop the strength, endurance, and technique to execute strokes correctly as well as awareness of their times. Now they must add to this a sense of pace. To do this they must memorize the sensations that result from a given amount of effort. Three techniques are used to develop this skill: descending sets, broken swims, and time trials.

Descending Sets

In a descending set, each distance in the set is swum faster than the previous distance. For example, "9 × 50 on 20 seconds rest, descend 1 through 3" is a descending set. The first time the set is given, the coach explains that team members are to swim 50 yards nine times with 20 seconds of rest after each 50. Team members would swim the third 50-yard length faster than the second and swim the second faster than the first. The same would be true of the fourth through the sixth and the seventh through the ninth sets. The comparison helps swimmers to memorize how their bodies feel at different speeds, and it encourages them to accelerate at the end of a swim.

Broken Swims

In broken swims, the distance a swimmer will swim in a race is divided into parts and a rest is given after each part. Broken swims should be related to goal times. They are introduced as follows: "8 × 100 on 1 minute rest. Break 10 seconds after each 25 yards. When you finish each 100 yards, subtract 30 seconds from your time and see how close you have come to your goal time." When your swimmers have completed this, they will know how it feels to swim each length at a pace that meets their goal times.

Time Trials

Time trials provide opportunities for your swimmers to compete against the clock in a race-like situation. Because swimmers will be starting from a dive, these events should be held at the end of practice on late season days when the atmosphere is warm. Use a stop watch, stand at the finish, and loudly call off the seconds that have elapsed since the start of the race. Tell your swimmers to lift their heads immediately after the finish in order to hear their times. They must realize that the times are accurate only to the nearest second, but the exercise will help them to memorize a swim at race pace. The three methods of developing a sense of pace require swimmers to be given longer rests between efforts than are given during midseason training. They also require a specific rest rather than the varied rest that results when a given time is stated for each effort, as, for example, 8 × 100 on 2 minutes.

Elements of Late Season Workouts

The following elements are typical of late season workouts:

1. Quality swims replace the endurance swims of the midseason. Swims for pace as well as all-out swims are stressed in late season workouts.
2. Longer rests are given between swims. The workouts will consist of approximately 50% repetition work. Interval work will be decreased. As a result, the number of yards swum will be reduced to between 2,500 and 3,000 for swimmers over the age of 10 and to 2,000 for swimmers under 10 years of age.
3. "Easy" swims are given for rest and as warmdowns. Although different speeds are designated during the early season and midseason, the swimmers are rarely told to swim "easy." In the late season, however, "easy" swims of approximately 200 yards are given after hard swims.
4. Swimmers are given choice of stroke as part of the late season workout. Swimmers should be aware of their own needs by late season, so the choice of stroke is frequently left to the swimmer.

The above changes are made over a period of 2 weeks. The swimmers' heads are now above water for longer periods of time, and these rest periods should be used to emphasize proper stroke techniques and to discuss the forthcoming late season competitions.

Creating a Healthy Attitude Toward Stress

Stress is an integral part of life and accompanies every challenge a youngster tries to meet. When stress is encountered in a situation that can be mastered, it is a positive factor for healthy development. As a coach, you have created a team that is important to your swimmers, and you have given them challenges to meet for their team. You must now teach your swimmers how to master the stress and the possible failure resulting from those challenges.

There are four things you can do to help your swimmers deal with both stress and possible failure. Most importantly, let your swimmers know that poor performances are simply that—poor performances and nothing more. They are not a measure of a swimmers' worth as a person. Secondly, have a positive attitude about every performance. Find good points about your swimmers' performances and indicate the good points, emphasizing that as long as your swimmers try, their performances are acceptable to you. Next help your swimmers to formulate realistic, achievable goals. Lastly, arrange for your swimmers to practice meeting challenges using one of the following methods.

Holding Times

A time to be swum and maintained throughout a workout or a *holding time* of 4 seconds above a best 50-yard time is realistic for a set with a long rest such as 8 × 50 on 2:30. To increase the stress, tell swimmers to rest for an additional 2:30 if they do not make their holding time and to count only the 50-yard lengths they swim below their holding times. If this challenge is given at the end of the workout, a few stragglers will be left still trying to make their holding times after their teammates have left the water. The coach must remain on the deck to encourage their attempts. Be sure these swimmers do not feel that they have failed but that, through perseverance, they have been successful.

Scoring Swims

Relate the workout to a golf game. Give the swimmers 9 × 100 on 4:00. Give them a goal time 7 seconds slower than their best 100-yard time. For each second under their goal time (par), they subtract 1 from their score; for each second over their goal time, they add 1 to par. For example, a swimmer who swims 100 yards in 1:02.0 would have a par of 69 (:62 + :07). The times for the first three swims might look like this:

Holding time	Actual time	Plus/Minus	Running score
69 (1:09)	67	−2	−2
69	69	0	−2
69	68	−1	−3

This swimmer would be swimming 3 under par for the first 3 × 100. Be sure to note the final scores and give recognition to the swimmers at or under par.

Elimination Relays

Relays are run near the end of the workout. Those swimmers who are on the winning relay are allowed to leave the workout immediately after the relay or to go off the high board or receive some other treat. The swimmers still in the workout do another set and then form their relay teams again so that the next winner can get out of the workout after that relay. Repeat this process until the last team is doing the final set. This device duplicates the team challenge that swimmers face at a meet. Be sure that the swimmers in the last relay know that you are not disappointed in them and be sure to point out the positive aspects of their swims.

By practicing dealing positively with both stress and possible failure, swimmers learn not to rate themselves as persons on the basis of how well they swim. Excuses, rejected compliments, or public displays of anger are signs that your swimmers are not handling stress well. You must help them to separate their swimming performance from their worth as human beings, to look for the positive aspect of each performance, and to accept themselves in defeat. When swimmers have learned to handle stress, they will enjoy competition more and compete more effectively.

The Taper: The Season's Fastest Swims

The time of the year when swimmers prepare to swim their fastest times is termed the *taper*. Coaches of college and year-round teams work within the following guidelines when preparing their swimmers for championship meets. These guidelines should be used only during the last 2 weeks before a championship meet and are applicable as adjusted to recreational teams.

Gradually decrease the total distance swum daily but maintain the same workout pattern. Your swimmers will probably attend ten practices during the last 2 weeks before the championship meet. A recreational team that has been swimming 4,000 yards a day during midseason could proceed as follows:

First 2 days.	Reduce total distance swum to 2,800 yards. Decrease interval work, increase repetition work, and include hypoxic sets.
Second 2 days.	Reduce total distance swum to 2,400 yards. Swimmers lose their timing during midseason and breathe too late in the crawl stroke and too early in the breaststroke. Use this time to perfect strokes and continue hypoxic work.
Third 2 days.	Reduce total distance swum to 2,000 yards. Work on sprint-

	ing, breathing patterns, and starts.
Fourth 2 days.	Reduce total distance swum to 1,600 yards. Improve turns.
Last 2 days.	Reduce total distance swum to 500 yards of easy swimming and kicking.

Work individually with your swimmers when possible. Be sure that you do not tire some swimmers by working them too hard or let others get out of shape.

The last days of the taper should be devoted to easy swimming with little or no sprinting. Use the extra time to emphasize the following instructions to your swimmers:

1. Don't lift the head to inhale directly after the dive.
2. Don't lift the head to inhale after the turn.
3. Push off on the side from turns.

Taper Atmosphere

Fun is a definite priority during the taper. Ensure that members of your club or school community are aware of the upcoming championship meet. A prize could be given for the best meet slogan, and a poster party could be held to prepare posters publicizing the team, the meet, or the meet slogan. Team cheers could be practiced, and if you ordered inexpensive items such as pins, balloons, hats, or banners, these could be distributed at this time. Get together with your team's older swimmers and ask them to plan this party. Direct them by telling them the purpose of the event but encourage them to use their own ideas and ingenuity.

Some international coaches introduce their swimmers to autosuggestion during the taper. You could suggest that just before sleeping at night your swimmers "see" and "feel" themselves swimming as they want to swim. Swimmers should mentally practice their strokes, turns, and starts as if they were swimming perfectly. Encourage your swimmers to swim their whole race mentally, starting with the command *Take your mark* and continuing the swim with the perfect number of breaths, a perfect turn, and a winning finish. Your swimmers' minds and bodies will thus practice the race through the power of suggestion.

Another mental drill that will help your swimmers is avoiding negative, harmful ideas such as "I can't win" and other self-defeating images. Immediately before and during the race itself, swimmers should concentrate on positive, helpful thoughts such as, "This is what I prepared for. The further I go, the easier it becomes." At the pool as the race time gets closer, swimmers should think of the high tempo and power of their stroking and the good judgment of their lap pace and feel certain that they will turn well. Do not allow your swimmers to waste their mental energy worrying about other competitors or the possibility of failure. The competitor's job is to achieve the optimal performance effort, and this task requires full concentration. Again, emphasize positive, helpful thoughts to your swimmers, not negative, harmful ones.

Activities in the water can also emphasize fun, team spirit, and positive feelings. Relays, a sharks and minnows game, or water volleyball (using a beach ball and the shallow end backstroke flags for a net) may be added to the regular workouts. Be sure to choose games that are safe and not excessively tiring. Enjoy these games with your swimmers when possible and remember that your attitude is still the key to creating a positive atmosphere and team spirit. Because you planned your team's goals in advance, gave your swimmers realistic goals, and helped them to achieve these goals, you should be able to enjoy this part of the season, and your enjoyment will be contagious.

Sample Late Season Workouts

Sample Workout 1

Swimmers:	Swimmers 10 years of age and under
Time in the water:	Approximately 1 hour
Yards swum:	2,000
Objectives:	To develop a sense of pace To perfect strokes To allow the coach to give individual swimmers assistance based on their specific interests.
Warm-Up: 1 × 250	Crawl, last 50 hard.
Kicking: 10 × 25 on :45	Swimmers' choice of stroke as long as it is legal.
Repetition Work: 8 × 50 on 2:00	Crawl. Descend 1-4.
8 × 50	Choice of any stroke except crawl. Descend 1-4.
Easy Swim: 1 × 150	Easy crawl.
Repetition Work: 4 × 100 on 1:00	:10 rest after each 25.
Easy Swim: 1 × 150	Easy crawl.

Sample Workout 2

Swimmers:	Swimmers 10 years of age and under
Time in the water:	60 minutes
Yards swum:	1,625
Objectives:	To review all strokes To provide work on strokes important to the swimmer To practice racing techniques
Warm-Up: 1 × 300	100 yards each of swim, kick, and pull. Break :10 after each 50.
Kicking: 4 × 100 with :30 rest	Individual medley order.
Interval Work: 8 × 25 with :20 rest	5 choice of the same stroke, 1 of each of the other strokes.
Repetition Work: 3 × 75 with 3:00 rest	Descend by 25s.
Interval Work: 1 × 400 rest as needed	No pressure for speed. Only 8 breaths on the even lengths.
Repetition Work: 4 × 25 rest as needed	Sprint from dive. 1 each stroke.

Sample Workout 3

Swimmers:	Swimmers over 10 years of age
Time in the water:	Approximately 1 hour, 20 minutes
Yards swum:	3,000
Objectives:	To develop a sense of pace To build confidence in speed To develop strengths and improve weaknesses on an individual basis
Warm-Up: 1 × 500	Crawl, negative split.
Kicking: 10 × 50 on 1:30	Choice of kick.
Repetition Work: 8 × 75 on 2:00	Crawl. Descend 1-4.
8 × 75 on 2:30	Any stroke but crawl. Descend 1-4.
Easy Swim: 1 × 200	Crawl easy.
Repetition Work: 4 × 100 with 1:00 rest	Crawl. Break :05 after 25 yards, :10 after 50 yards, and :15 after 75 yards. Subtract :30 at end to get 100 time.
Easy Swim: 1 × 200	Easy crawl.

Sample Workout 4

Swimmers:	Swimmers over 10 years of age
Time in the water:	1 hour, 20 minutes
Yards swum:	12,550
Objectives:	To develop race pace To learn to swim hard at end of race
Warm-Up: 1 × 300	100 yards each of swim, kick, and pull.
Interval Work: 8 × 50 with :20 rest	Two different strokes, swimmer's choice. Descend so that each is :01 faster than the previous one.
Repetition Work: 8 × 100 with :30 rest	Individual medleys. Descend so that each is :01 faster than the previous one.
3 × 150 with 3:00 rest	Descend each 50 of the 150. Choice of stroke
Easy Swim: 500	No pressure for speed, but only 6 breaths on the even lengths.
Repetition Work: 4 × 25	Sprint from a dive for time. 1 of each stroke.

Evaluating Your Progress

1. Which of the following methods are not used to establish a sense of pace?

   a. Descending sets
   b. Stroke work
   c. Broken swims
   d. Monsters
   e. Time trials

2. List three objectives of the late season and taper.
3. Describe the differences between midseason and late season training.
4. What can the coach do to help swimmers accomplish their best times?
5. Describe the coach's role when swimmers fail to meet a challenge.

Chapter 10: Coaching at Meets

At the conclusion of this chapter, you should be able to employ the correct information to maximize your effectiveness in preparing for and coaching at meets, including the following:

- Preparing for the first home meet.
- Preparing for all meets.
- Coaching at the warm-up.
- Helping your team during the meet.
- Concluding a meet.

A well-run and well-coached meet will help sell your program and will be a beneficial experience for swimmers. It also offers parents an opportunity to see what their children are learning and potential swimmers an opportunity to consider the advantages of becoming a member of your team. Therefore, it is essential that competitive swim meets be run smoothly and that you be available to your swimmers at this time. Premeet planning is the key to this accomplishment.

Before the First Home Meet

Before the first home meet, hold a dress rehearsal. If the parents have traditionally conducted meets, hold an intrasquad meet before the first home meet. Following this intrasquad meet, talk with the meet director to make suggestions to improve the way meets are conducted to benefit the swimmers.

If the policy of your team is to pay officials, hire and notify them well in advance and determine and arrange for the equipment you are supposed to supply. In addition, review the directions for meet personnel and for conducting meets as described in the appropriate rule book. Read these directions again even if you read them during the previous season.

Also hold a short team meeting to discuss swimmers' conduct at meets. Tell your swimmers that they are expected to sit with their team, not their parents. If possible, describe the team's general seating area at the meet site. Team members may cheer during a race, but not between the time when the whistle is blown and the gun is fired to signal the start of the race.

Swimmers should be courteous to officials at all times. Only the coach should talk with officials regarding controversial decisions. Swimmers will be notified regarding the race in which they will swim at least four events before the race. Although the coach will discuss different events with each swimmer, effective meet strategy requires swimmers not to be notified of a definite decision too far in advance. After an event, each swimmer will get his or her official time and report it to the coach's assistant.

Swimmers should always be given a premeet warm-up. If possible, inform the swimmers of the specific lanes they are to use for warming up.

You must also select relay participants for the meet. Coaches usually find themselves with swimmers vying for limited relay spots. Develop and announce your policy for choosing relay swimmers before the first meet. One successful policy for selecting relay participants is to select those swimmers with the fastest recorded time for the stroke and distance for the relay. Faster swims on the day of the meet may lead to changes in the premeet relay designs.

Also discuss with your team the goals to be achieved at the meet. Stress to your swimmers that the use of proper racing skills is one of your highest goals for this meet. You may add other pertinent factors such as the opposing team's win and loss record against your team or other teams in your league or the number of "best times" you would like to see at this meet.

Before Every Meet

Home meets and away meets present different problems because you are both coach and administrator. Thus, organizing and delegating work will be important for you.

Preparing the Meet Entries and Entry Cards

During preseason, you should have established a system with a parent or manager to record each swimmer's performance record on a card. Through either time trials or previous meets, you have recorded your swimmers' times for pertinent events on these cards. Now make a chart listing the swimmers' names on the left and the events for the age group across the top. The example coach's sheet given in Figure 10-1 and provided in Appendix #B is for an age-group meet held in a six-lane pool. It is for the 11- and 12-year-old age group only. In this instance, the participation limitation states that competitors may enter two events and a relay. This requirement does not prohibit a swimmer from entering two relays and one other event. Using the cards and observing the participation rule, enter each swimmer's time opposite the event and the swimmer's name. In an age-group meet, make a sheet for each age group. For a high school meet, use only one sheet.

When you have selected the participants for the meet, you are ready to prepare the entry cards. The league or home team should supply the coaches with an individual entry card for each swimmer in each event. The coaches fill out these cards in advance of the meet when possible, but sometimes you may need to fill in the lanes on the day of the meet. The swimmers take these cards to the lane timers before swimming an event, and the timer uses the card to record the swimmers' official times (see Figure 10-2).

An alternative system requires the use of a single card for each event. All contestants from the team are listed on this card, and it is turned in by the coach before the event (see Figure 10-3).

Appointing an Assistant

Appoint an assistant to fill out cards, when necessary, to record the swimmers' times, record the swimmers' splits (i.e., the time for the race broken into laps), and record any comments the coach may wish to pass onto the swimmers.

The Meet Warm-Up

During the time provided for the meet warm-up, you should conduct an orientation meeting to gear your swimmers up for the meet and provide sufficient time for your swimmers to warm up.

Team Orientation Meeting

During the time provided for warm up at the meet, hold a team meeting and announce the following:

- Where your team will sit.
- The lanes your swimmers will warm up in.
- The lanes they will be racing in. If possible, swimmers should race in the same lanes they warm up in.
- The skills they should work on during the warm-up, including the following:
  1. Counting the number of strokes from the "T" to the wall for front turns.
  2. Counting the number of strokes from the flags to the wall for backstroke turns.
- Adjustments the swimmers will want to make for pool differences at any away meet. Look for the following:
  1. Lack of depth at the shallow end.
  2. Slippery walls.
  3. Starting blocks that are unstable. Unstable starting blocks can be corrected by having

Fig. 10-1

COACH'S SHEET
11 & 12's

EVENT NUMBERS BOYS	3	13	23	33	43	53
11 & 12 year olds	200 medley relay	50 crawl	50 back	50 breast	25 fly	400 free relay
Jim Jones	Back 40.2		40.2		15.3	
John White	Breast 48.1			48.1		
Charlie Johns	Fly 39.1		39.1		15.0	
Jeff Murphy	Free 32.3	32.3				1:10.0
Tom O'Brien		33.1			16.8	1:10.2
Rick Tobias		35.2		48.5		1:11.0
Dick Johns			42.0	49.1		1:09.0

EVENT NUMBERS GIRLS	4	14	24	34	44	54
Wendy Johns	Fly 38.1		44.3		18.0	
Cheryl Klyski	Crawl 34.1	34.1			19.1	
Karen Zol	Breast 50.2		47.6	50.2		
Maura Cost		35.1			18.5	1:12.1
Meg Sparks		36.1		51.0		1:14.0
Dotty Jacks						1:15.0
Chris Haggers	Back 41.2		41.2			1:13.0

Fig. 10-2

INDIVIDUAL ENTRY CARD

EVENT# __________
EVENT __________
LANE# __________
NAME __________
TEAM __________
PLACE __________

Fig. 10-3

TEAM ENTRY CARD

EVENT __________
SCHOOL __________
NAME __________ LANE #____
NAME __________ LANE #____
NAME __________ LANE #____
JUDGE'S INITIALS __________

a teammate sit on the back of the block at the start.

4. Lack of a place to grab for the start. Use a relay start if this is a problem.
5. Lack of gutters at the turning ends.

The Meet Warm-Up

Divide your team evenly in assigned lanes to warm up. This should start with easy crawl stroke. It should include kicking followed by swimming each racing stroke. During the general warm-up, swimmers do not stop to practice starts. Starts are usually practiced after the warm-up by doing no more than three one-length sprints on a command *Go* from the coach. Swimmers under 10 years of age should practice the start and then swim hard to the first set of flags, easy between the flags, and hard from the second set of flags to the wall. The distance portion of the meet warm-up should be approximately 800 yards for swimmers over 10 years of age and 200 to 300 yards for younger swimmers. The following are examples of premeet warm-ups:

- For older swimmers:

  1 × 300 crawl

  2 × 100 kick using any kick swimmers might be asked to swim in the meet.

  4 × 50 using the swimmer's choice of any stroke he or she might have to swim in the meet.

  100 easy swim, choice of stroke.

- For younger swimmers:

  2 × 50 easy crawl.

  1 × 50 kick, choice of kick.

  4 ×25 swim, 1 length of each stroke ending with crawl.

During the Meet

Once competition begins you can easily focus on the excitement of the meet. However, because you are the coach you must focus your attention onto your particular swimmers and helping them have a successful and rewarding experience.

Watch for Common Racing Errors

During the meet, watch your swimmers for common racing errors, including the following:

1. Holding the breath too long during the first portion of the race creates an oxygen debt that exhausts the swimmer for the last portion of the race.
2. Lifting the head after the dive is usually accompanied by a breath and is probably done to see where the opponents are. Unfortunately, the swimmer loses the momentum from the dive with this movement.
3. Shortening the stroke is usually an effort to swim faster. The swimmer strokes quickly and forgets to push the stroke all the way through, thus losing power and momentum.

Talk With Swimmers as They Report Their Times

Keep your comments to your swimmers' positive by mentioning the good features of a swimmers' race before discussing the items that need further improvement. During the meet, do not discuss any corrections that do not pertain to events to be swum later that day. Those items should be written down and discussed later at practice.

Take Swimmers' Splits

You will need a split watch to take your swimmers' splits. With this type of watch, you can stop the time long enough to read the time for a portion of the race while also keeping track of the running time in the race. There is probably not enough time for the coach to record these times and still perform the other necessary duties. Therefore, read these times to an assistant. Information of this kind is helpful to older swimmers when they are trying to pace their races evenly. It also shows the individual medley swimmers the strokes on which they need more work.

Organize Relays

Although your relay squads are selected in advance, make changes if desirable when one swimmer is able to swim a better time than an established relay swimmer.

After the Meet

After the meet, call your swimmers together to cheer their opponents. Then sit them down to talk about the good aspects of their performance in the meet. All comments at this time should be positive, with emphasis on swimmers who improved their performances in comparison with their own previous efforts. Later, you should review the comments recorded by the meet assistant and restructure practice sessions to emphasize areas of your swimmers' performances that appeared to be weak during the meet.

Evaluating Your Progress

1. What is your policy for choosing relay swimmers?
2. List the possible pool variations coaches of visiting teams should look for and discuss with their swimmers.
3. List the duties of the coach before a meet.
4. List the duties of the coach during a meet.
5. List the duties of the coach directly after a meet.

Appendix A: Answer Pages For Evaluating Your Progress

Chapter 2

1. a
2. b
3. a. "High elbows."
   b. "Exhale while your face is in the water."
   c. "Kick from the hips."
4. b
5. b
6. a
7. a
8. a
9. b

Chapter 3

1. c
2. c
3. c
4. c
5. 2 Arm pull
   1 Start of kicking motion
   3 Head positioning
6. b
7. Hands one on top of the other
   Head between the arms
   Stretch

Chapter 4

1. c
2. b
3. b
4. a
5. c
6. b
7. No

Chapter 5

1. b
2. a
3. b
4. c
5. c

Chapter 6

1. What is the background of the potential swimmers?
   What is the pool time allotted to the team?
   How many swimmers are expected to participate?
   In what league will the team compete, and who determines the rules for the league?
2. a. Taper
   b. Early season
   c. Early season
   d. Midseason
   e. Early season
   f. Taper
   g. Late season

3. To offer healthy activity.
   To encourage mental and physical discipline.
   To recognize accomplishments.
   To provide opportunity for social adjustment and exposure.
   To offer a constructive use of leisure time.
   To develop potential talent.
4. Attendance, point, and conduct requirements.
5. Absences for acceptable reasons should be requested in advance. Universally accepted excuses include illness, death in the family, need to report for extra help after school. Most coaches also accept dentist or physician appointments, family vacations, and family illness.
6. Point system established in advance. Give points for attendance at practice, leadership, points in dual meets, points in championship meets, and team or league records held.
7. Lane lines, backstroke flags, pace clock, kick boards, materials for running meets, bulletin boards, record board, and written materials.

Chapter 7

1. The coach can assist the swimmer by
   providing positive feedback on the goals.
   providing information relevant to the goals.
   providing the time frame for the goal's accomplishment.
2. Possible answer for a swimmer who has chosen a goal that is too difficult: "This goal is a long-term goal. It is one you can accomplish if you continue swimming after this season by joining a year-round club. Have you thought about what you must do to qualify for the league championships?"

   Possible answer for a swimmer who has chosen a goal that the coach believes is too easy: "The goal of qualifying for the league championships is certainly realistic, but do you know that the league record is close to the time you swam in practice last week? Let's check the record and think about how fast you could go if you improved your turns by our next meet."
3. Prepare a list of the exercises before the session.
   Check that the athletes are doing the exercises correctly.
   Explain the purpose of the exercises.
4. Exercises should be done every other day.
   Precede each session with a warm-up.
   Use the muscles in the same motion and rhythm that they will be used for swimming.
   Overload the muscle.
   Try to motivate swimmers by doing exercises with them.
   Encourage swimmers to be patient. Strength increase takes 4 to 6 weeks of training.
   Exercises must be done correctly.
   Develop power as well as strength.
5. Have swimmers do strength exercises hard and fast.
6. b
7. b
8. b
9. Jumps in place, partner squats.
10. Stay to the right of the midline.
    Cut to the middle just before the turn.
    Let faster swimmers pass on the turns.
11. c
12. The five elements of an early season workout are: (a) stretching, (b) warm-up, (c) stroke work, (d) interval training, (e) repetition work.

Chapter 8

1. c
2. b
3. Never repeat a workout.
   Don't tell swimmers what the workout will be until they are ready to begin.
   Give special instructions with each set.
   Vary the strokes.
   Play games.
4. Allow swimmers in some lanes to rest during parts of sets.
   Give a timed swim to see how many lengths can be swum in a specific time.
   Give faster swimmers slower strokes.
   Give slower swimmers shorter lengths to swim with the same interval.

5. Swimmers should use legal turns.
   Swimmers should finish each length hard.
   Swimmers should streamline off walls.
   Swimmers should use efficient strokes.
   Face in the water where applicable.
6. Publicize meets, invite alumni, and publish meet schedules.

Chapter 9

1. b (strokework),
   d (monsters).
2. Establish a sense of pace.
   Help swimmers to swim their best times.
   Have fun.
3. Fewer yards are swum in late season.
   More stroke work done in late season.
   More quality work done in late season.
   Some easy swims are assigned in late season.
   Choice of stroke is given more often in late season.
4. Prepare swimmers psychologically.
   Prepare swimmers physically.
5. Find something good in the swimmer's performance.
   Let your swimmer know that his value as a person is not based on swimming performance.
   Consider what can be done right the next time to improve performance.

Chapter 10

1. Fastest recorded time.
2. Slippery starting blocks, backstroke flags, "T"s, blocks, or gutters that are different from those in the home pool.
3. Ensure that meet committees have proper equipment and officials.
   Ensure that swimmers know what to do at the meet.
   Ensure that swimmers have proper goals.
   Prepare the meet entries and entry cards.
   Ensure that you have someone willing to assist with record keeping.
4. Watch for racing errors.
   Talk with swimmers before and after swims.
   Take splits and make relays.
5. Meet with swimmers to discuss positive aspects of their performances and encourage cheering.

Appendix B: Coaching Swimming Effectively Evaluation

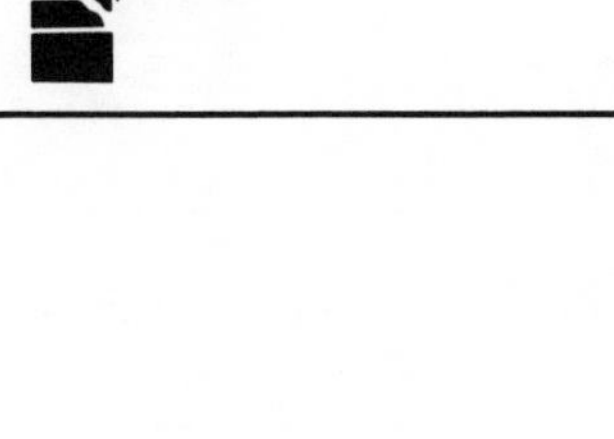

Tell Us What You Think

It is our commitment at ACEP to provide coaches with the most complete, accurate, and useful information available. Our authors, consultants, and editors are continuously searching for new ideas and are constantly seeking to improve our materials. Now that you have read and studied this book, it is your turn to tell us what you liked and did not like about it. Please take a few minutes to complete the following survey and send it to: ACEP, Box 5076, Champaign, IL 61820.

Book Evaluation for *Coaching Swimming Effectively*

Instructions: For each statement mark the spaces in the left-hand column which correspond to what you think of this book. We are interested in your opinions so feel free to mark more than one response to each statement.

1. The organization of this book

___ (a) presents material in an easy-to-understand progression
___ (b) is helpful
___ (c) is confusing

2. The material presented in this book is

___ (a) easy to read and understand
___ (b) difficult to read and understand
___ (c) too simple
___ (d) too complex

3. Figures and illustrations are

___ (a) helpful
___ (b) distracting
___ (c) technically correct
___ (d) technically incorrect
___ (e) confusing

4. Coaching points and teaching progressions

___ (a) highlight material in the book well
___ (b) progress from basic to advanced concepts
___ (c) are helpful
___ (d) are distracting
___ (e) are too repetitive

5. Drills

___ (a) need illustrations
___ (b) are helpful
___ (c) are confusing
___ (d) are too advanced for beginning swimmers
___ (e) are too simple for beginning swimmers
___ (f) are easy to use
___ (g) are difficult to use

6. Instructional schedules are

___ (a) helpful
___ (b) easy to understand
___ (c) difficult to understand

7. Practice plans are

___ (a) helpful
___ (b) confusing
___ (c) too basic
___ (d) too advanced
___ (e) easy to use
___ (f) difficult to use

8. Coaching aids are

___ (a) helpful
___ (b) not helpful
___ (c) easy to use
___ (d) difficult to use

Yes No

___ **9. I feel more knowledgeable about coaching swimming to beginning swimmers than I did before reading this book.**

___ **10. I would like to attend a workshop or clinic covering the material presented in this book.**

Glossary

Anchor. The swimmer to swim the last leg on a relay team.

Backstroke Flags. A line of flags stretched across the pool 15 feet inside each end of the course to help backstrokers know when they are approaching the wall.

Broken Swims. A form of training that requires a long swim to be broken into shorter swims. A 200-yard swim may be broken four times at the 50-yard mark or once at each 100-yard mark. Swimmers try to swim progressively faster with each part of a broken swim or to add their times up to equal a best time.

Cardiovascular Endurance. The ability of the heart and blood vessels to continue supplying blood to the muscles at a given rate of intensity.

Concentric Contraction. The shortening and contracting of a muscle sufficiently to overcome a resistance.

Descending Set. A number of short swims with each distance swum faster than the previous distance.

Dolphin Kick. The kick used in the butterfly stroke. The feet move up and down together, simulating the movement of a dolphin.

Disqualification. Being eliminated from competition due to incorrect stroke, turn, or start.

Early Season. The first 30% of the swimming season when basic skills and stroke work are emphasized.

Endurance. The relative ability to continue exercising at a given rate of intensity for a specified length of time.

False Start. If a swimmer moves or leaves the starting blocks too soon, a false start is called. It is signaled by two shots from the starter's gun. Rules stipulate that after a specific number of false starts, the competitor is disqualified.

Flexibility. The range of motion within the various joints of the body.

Flip. A commonly used tumbling turn. The swimmer bends and twists the body and then pushes off the wall with the feet to accomplish the turn.

Freestyle Relay. A race including many swimmers swimming freestyle in succession.

Goggles. Equipment worn over the eyes to allow swimmers to see while keeping the water out of the eyes.

Gutter Push-Ups. An exercise performed by swimmers placing both hands on the gutter directly in front of the shoulders. They push up until the elbows are straight and then lower themselves until the elbows are straight.

Grab Start. A start commonly used in the freestyle, butterfly, or breaststroke. The swimmer starts from a forward bending position by grabbing the starting block.

Holding Time. Swimming time to be maintained throughout workout. Usually certain number of seconds slower than swimmer's best time for the distance swum.

Hypoxic Training. Training drills that restrict breathing and thus make less oxygen available to the cells.

Interval Training. A training method that allows a set distance to be repeated with a very short rest. Time of the rest is not enough to allow full recovery.

Individual Medley. A race requiring a competitor to swim an equal distance of the four competitive strokes in the following order: butterfly, backstroke, breaststroke, and freestyle.

IM. An abbreviation swimmers often use to refer to the individual medley.

Isometric Contraction. An exercise in which a muscle is contracted without motion against a stationary resistance.

Kickboard. A lightweight board used by swimmers for support while practicing kicking drills.

Lane Lines. Floats that run the length of the pool to mark the boundaries of the lane. In some cases the lines will calm the waves.

Lane Markers. Dark lines on the bottom of the pool that mark the center of each lane. They usually have markings to warn the swimmer that he is close to the wall, and they help the swimmer to swim straight.

Length. Distance of the pool from end to end.

Medley Relay. A relay race including four swimmers, one for each of the competitive strokes in the following order: backstroke, breaststroke, butterfly, and freestyle.

Midseason. The middle portion of the season when endurance work is stressed.

Natural Breaststroke. A legal, acceptable breaststroke typified by a high breath and up-and-down hip action.

Overload Principle. The term used to indicate that the body must be stressed beyond a normal operating level in order to gain positive benefits. Swimmers must swim longer and harder to improve endurance and speed.

Pace. The rate that a competitor swims a race or portion of a race.

Pace Clock. A large clock with a second hand used for training.

Pike. Keeping the legs straight and the hips flexed.

Pull. A training technique that uses only the arms for the force to propel the swimmer through the water.

Record. The fastest recorded time in a particular event. There are world records, American records, team records, and age group records, all of which are the fastest times done in the stated group.

Recovery. The sweep of a swimmer's arm when it returns to the catch position.

Recreational Competitive Teams. Teams that swim a season running from 2 to 6 months each year, engage primarily in dual meets, and swim an adjusted format of events stressing the shorter distances.

Referee. The official with full jurisdiction over the meet. The main duty of the referee is to enforce all rules.

Relay. An event that requires many individuals to swim one after another.

Relay Start. A start preceded by a wind up of the arms and used by swimmers on a relay.

Split. An intermediate section of a race. The split time shows the length of time taken to swim a particular section of the race.

Sprint. The shortest distance in each stroke.

Starter. The person who has control of the start of each race and who recalls the swimmers in the event of a false start.

Streamlining. Stretching the body in such a way that it offers the least possible resistance to the water.

Strength. The relative capacity of a muscle to exert force against an external resistance.

Stroke Judge. An official who watches swimmers' strokes to see that they are done according to the rules.

Sweat Suit. Colorful pants and jackets worn to keep a swimmer warm and comfortable between events. These should be worn every time the swimmer leaves the water.

Taper. The end of the swimming season when swimmers prepare to swim their fastest times.

Time Trials. Practice opportunity for swimmers to be timed under simulated race conditions.

Traditional Breaststroke. The breaststroke taught to beginners in most swimming lessons. This emphasizes a flat body position.

Turn Judge. An official who stands at the end of a lane and watches swimmers' turns to see that they are done according to the rules.

Warm-up. The period, usually an hour to an hour and a half before the start of a meet, when competitors accustom themselves to the pool, warm up their muscles, and practice starts and turns. This term may also signify the wearing apparel worn over the bathing suit to keep the muscles warm.

Resources

Bibliography Techniques and Information for Recreational Programs

Altman, R. (Fall 1975) "Training the Novice Swim Team." *Swimming Technique*, pp. 82-86.

American National Red Cross. (1981). *Swimming and aquatics safety.* Washington, DC: Author.

Counsilman, J. (1979). *The complete book of swimming.* New York: Atheum.

Firby, H. (1979). Fundamentals of butterfly for novice swimmers. *American Swimming Coaches Association world clinic yearbook.* Fort Lauderdale, FL: ASCA.

Gabrielson, Milton, Spears, Betty, Gabrielson, J. (1968). *Aquatics Handbook.* Englewood Cliffs: Prentice Hall.

Kamberg, M.L. (1979, May-June). When your swimmers are long on energy but short on basics. *Swimmers Coach*, pp. 27-34.

National Federation of State High School Associations. (1982). *Official High School Swimming and Diving, Water Polo Rules.* Kansas City, MO: Author.

Snyder, R. (1978, June-August). Programs at Wilson High School. *Swimmer's*, pp. 12-16.

Young, R. (1979). Fun in age group programs. *American Swimming Coaches Association world clinic yearbook.* Fort Lauderdale, FL: ASCA.

Techniques and Information for Year-Round Programs

Carlisle, F. (1963). *Forbes Carlisle on swimming.* London: Pelham.

Colwin, C. (1977). *An introduction to swimming coaching.* Ottawa: Canadian Amateur Swimming Association.

Counsilman, J.E. (1968). *The science of swimming.* Englewood Cliffs, NJ: Prentice-Hall.

Counsilman, J.E. (1977). *Competitive swimming manual for coaches and swimmers.* Bloomington, IN: Counsilman, Inc.

Wilkie, D. (1978). *Winning with Wilkie: A guide to better swimming.* London: Hutchinson.

Coaching Philosophy and Attitude

Goforth, J. (1979). Motivating swimmers. *American Swimming Coaches Association World Clinic Yearbook.* Fort Lauderdale, FL: ASCA.

Jacklin, D. (1973, March). Working together for kids and for life. *Swimming World*, pp. 23-25.

Tutko, T. & Richards, J. (1972). *A coach's practical guide to athletic motivation.* Boston: Allyn Bacon.

Dryland Exercise Information

Dawson, B. (1974). *The complete book of dry land exercise for swimming.* London: Pelham.

Falls, H.B., Baylor, A.M. & Dishman, R.K. (1982). *Essentials of fitness.* Philadelphia: Sanders.